TIBET
THE HEART OF ASIA

TIBET
THE HEART OF ASIA

BY
NICHOLAS ROERICH

GYAN

Published by

GYAN

Gyan Publishing House
5, Ansari Road
Daryaganj, New Delhi-110002
Phone: 011-47034999, 9811692060
E-mail: books@gyanbooks.com

Distribution Network
gyanbooks.com
India, USA, Canada, UK, Australia, France

ISBN : 978-81-212-2913-5 (PB)
First Published, 1930

2nd Impression 2021

Printed at: Gyan Press, Delhi.

Tibet: The Heart of Asia
Author: Nicholas Roerich

HEART OF ASIA

By NICHOLAS ROERICH

NEW ERA LIBRARY

ROERICH MUSEUM PRESS

NEW YORK MCMXXX

PUBLISHER'S NOTE

In presenting the Heart of Asia as the first volume in the Light of Asia Series in the New Era Library, we are transmitting the synthesis of Roerich's impression of the East, and his deep understanding of that great spirit which has gestated in turn each religion of the world. Professor Roerich here crystallizes the past and the future hope of the heart of Asia.

CONTENTS

Part I

Part II

PART I

THE HEART OF ASIA

I

THE HEART OF ASIA

IS THE heart of Asia beating? Or is it suffocated by the sands?

From the Brahmaputra to the Irtysh, from the Yellow River to the Caspian Sea, from Mukden to Arabia—everywhere are terrific, merciless waves of sand. The cruel Taklamakan is a threatening apotheosis of lifelessness, deadening the central part of Asia. In moving sands, the old Imperial Chinese road hides itself. Out of sandy hills, trunks of an erstwhile mighty forest, lift their seared arms. Like deformed skeletons, the age-devoured walls of ancient cities stretch along the road.

Perhaps along this very spot passed the great travelers, the migrating nations. The eye, here and there, glimpses isolated kereksurs, menhirs, cromlechs and rows of stones, silent guardians of ancient cults.

The extremities of Asia, to be certain, wage a gigantic struggle with the tides of the ocean. But is the heart alive? When Hindu Yogi arrest their pulse, their heart still continues its inner functions. Thus, also, is it with the heart of Asia. In oases, in yurtas, in caravans, dwells a peculiar thought. The masses of people, entirely isolated from the outside world, who receive some distorted message of outside events only after a lapse of months, do not die. Each sign of civilization, as we shall see, is greeted by them, like a benevolent, long awaited message. Rather than reject possibilities, they try to coördinate their religions with the new conditions of life. This is apparent when we see what the people in the most remote deserts say of the leaders of civilization and humanitarianism.

The name of Ford, for instance, has penetrated into the most remote yurtas and provinces.

Amidst the sands of the Taklamakan, a long-bearded Moslem asks: "Say, could a Ford pass the old Chinese road?"

And near Kashgar they ask: "Can a Ford tractor plow our fields?"

In Chinese Urumchi, in the Kalmuck steppes, throughout Mongolia, the word "Ford" is used as a synonym for motive power.

A gray-bearded Old Believer in the wild Altai mountains, as well as a youth of the Coöperative, says enviously: "In America, you have a Ford. But unfortunately we have none" . . . Or, "If only Ford were here."

Even in the Tibetan highlands, they dream of carrying a Ford in parts, up through the mountain passes.

Crossing powerful streams, they ask: "But could your Ford cross this?"

Ascending steep slopes, they ask again: "And could a Ford also climb up here?"—as if they were speaking of some fairy giant, who can surmount all obstacles.

And another American name has penetrated into the most secluded spots: in a far-away corner of the Altai, in a peasant's hut, in the most venerated corner where the sacred images are kept, one may recognize a familiar face—a yellowish portrait, apparently taken from some stray magazine. Looking closer, you see that it is none other than President Hoover himself. The Old Believer says:

"This is he, who feeds the people. Yes, there exist such rare, remarkable persons, who not only feed their own nation, but even other people. Yet the mouth of the people is not a small one."

The old man himself had never received an A. R. A. food package, but the living legend has crossed rivers and mountains, proclaiming how the generous giant kindheartedly distributed food and nourished the nations of the entire world.

One would never expect that news from the outside world could penetrate to the outskirts of Mongolia. But in a forsaken yurta a Mongol again tells you that somewhere beyond the ocean there lives a great man, who feeds all starving people. And he pronounces a name in a rather strange way, sounding somewhat like Hoover or Koovera—the Buddhist Deity of wealth and good fortune. In the most unexpected places, a traveler who has mastered the local language, can encounter inspiring legends about the great people working for the good of all.

Through the Rockefeller Institutions, the name of Rockefeller has also reached even far-off cities. With pride and satisfaction, the people speak of their collaboration with these institutions and the way they have been helped in this name. The generosity of this American hand has created a direct, widespread feeling of gratitude and friendship.

The fourth outstanding cultural name widely known in the spaces of Asia, is that of Senator Borah. A letter from him is regarded as a good passport everywhere. Sometimes in Mongolia, or in the Altai, or in Chinese Turkestan, you may hear a strange pronunciation of this name: "Boria is a powerful man!"

In this way, popular wisdom evaluates the great leaders of our times. This is so valuable to hear. So precious is it to know that human evolution, by undescribed paths, penetrates the future.

Everywhere, the American Banner accompanied us, fastened to a Mongolian spear. It accompanied us through Sinkiang, through the Mongolian Gobi, through Tsaidam and through Tibet. It was our standard during the encounter with the wild Panagis. It greeted the Tibetan governors, princes and their generals. Many friends did it meet, and but few enemies. And these latter few were even of quite a special type: the governor of the northern Tibetan fortress Nag-Chu, who assured us that there were only seven nations in all the world. Another was Ma, the Taotai of Khotan, who was a complete ignoramus and who is renowned for his murders.

But the friends were numerous. If only the West could see with what intense interest all photographs of New York skyscrapers were examined, and how hungrily the people listened to our narratives of life in America, it would rejoice to hear how such masses of simple people are attracted to cultural achievements.

Of course in a brief survey we cannot tell in detail of the whole of Central Asia. But even in fragmentary characteristics, we may still review the contemporary situation of those vast lands and glance at the monuments of a heroic past as well as the untold riches of Asia.

As everywhere, on one side you can see remarkable monuments, refined processes of thought based on the ancient wisdom and the cordiality of human relationship. You can rejoice at beauty and can easily be understood. But do not be astonished to find, in the very same places, perverted forms of religions, ignorance, signs of decay and degeneration.

We must take things at their true value. Without conventional sentimentality, we must greet the light and justly expose pernicious darkness. We must carefully discriminate prejudice and superstition from the hidden symbols of ancient knowledge. Let us greet all which aspires towards creation and construction and deplore the barbaric destruction of the treasures of nature and of the spirit.

Of course, as an artist my main aspiration in Asia was towards artistic work, and it is even difficult to estimate how soon I can embody all my artistic impressions and sketches—so generous are these gifts of Asia. No knowledge acquired in literature or in museums empowers one to express Asia or any other country, unless he has seen it with his own eyes and unless he has made at least some notes and sketches on the sites themselves.

Conviction, this magic and intangible property of creation, comes only in the continuous cumulation of real conceptions. It is true, mountains everywhere are mountains, water everywhere is water, sky everywhere is sky, and men everywhere are men. But nevertheless, if seated before the Alps, you attempt to picture the Himalayas, something inexplicable but convincing will be lacking.

In addition to its artistic aims, our Expedition planned to study the position of the ancient monuments of Central Asia, to observe the present condition of religions and creeds, and to note the traces of the great migrations of nations. This latter problem has always been of special interest to me. In the latest discoveries of the Kosloff expedition, in the works of Professors Rostovtseff, Borovka, Makarenko, Toll and many others, we see the great interest in Scythian, Mongolian and Gothic antiquities. The ancient discoveries in Siberia, the traces of the great migrations in Minusinsk, Altai, Ural, add an extraordinarily rich artistic and historic material to the Pan-European Romanesque and early Gothic. And how close these themes are to contemporary artistic creation—many of these animal and floral stylizations might have come from the best modern workshop.

* * *

The main route of the Expedition widely encircled Central Asia. The chief points to be mentioned were the following:

Darjeeling, the monasteries of Sikkim, Benares, Sarnath, Northern Punjab, Rawalpindi, Kashmir, Ladak,

Karakorum, Khotan, Yarkend, Kashgar, Aksu, Kuchar, Karashahr, Toksun, the Turfan region, Urumchi, T'ien-Shan, Kozeun, Zaisan, Irtysh, Novonikolaevsk, Biisk, Altai, Oirotia, Verkhneudinsk, Buriatya, Troitskosavsk, Altyn-Bulak, Urga, Yum-Beise, Anhsi-chou, Shih-pao ch'eng, Nanshan, Sharagolji, Tsaidam, Neiji, Marco Polo range, Kokushili, Dungbure, Nagchu, Shentsa-Dzong, Tingri-Dzong, Shekar-Dzong, Kampa-Dzong, Sepo La, Gangtok, and back to Darjeeling.

We crossed the following mountain passes. We have a list of thirty-five passes from fourteen to twenty-one thousand feet:

Zoji La, Khardong La, Karaul Davan, Sasser Pass, Dabzang Pass, Karakorum Pass, Suget Pass, Sanju Pass, Urtu-Kashkariym Daban, Ulan Daban, Chakharin Daban, Khentu Pass, Neiji La, Kokushili Pass, Dungbure Pass, Thang La, Kam-rong La, Ta-sang La, Lamsi Pass, Naptra La, Tamaker Pass, Shentsa Pass, Laptse-Nagri, Tsang La, Lam-Ling Pass, Pong-chen La, Dong-chen La, Sang-mo La, Kyegong La, Tsug-chung La, Gya La, Urang La, Sharu La, Gulung La and Sepo La.

While speaking of the crossing of the passes, it may be mentioned that, except on the Thang La, during the entire journey with its many passes, no one suffered seriously. Even in the case of the Thang La, the conditions were exceptional. There was a feeling of nervousness in the Expedition over the uncertain negotiations with the Tibetans. The conditions of the pass itself are also most exacting. George had such an exhausting heart attack there, that he almost fell from his horse. Our doctor administered large doses of digitalis and ammonia and, expressing anxiety for his life, restored the blood circulation by massage. Lama Malonoff also fell from his horse there and was found lying unconscious on the ground. Besides this, three more members of the caravan had serious attacks of "Soor" or mountain sickness which is evident in headache, poor blood circulation, sickness and general fatigue. In any case, such weakness, in a varying degree, is characteristic during the crossing of the mountain passes. On the passes bleeding often sets in, first from the nose and later from other less protected organs.

The same symptoms may also be seen with animals at altitudes of fifteen thousand feet. The caravan road through Kardong, Sasser, Karakorum, especially is covered with skeletons of all sorts of animals: horses, donkeys, mules, yaks, camels and dogs. On the way we saw several weak animals heavily bleeding, which had been left behind. Motionless and trembling, they awaited their end. Their death could not be averted. There would have been only one way to save them: to take them away from the altitude of seventeen or eighteen thousand feet, to an altitude of about seven or eight thousand, which was impossible. In our caravan we had cases of bleeding among the men and animals, but fortunately without any disastrous results. Probably the measures which we took each time before crossing a pass, prevented this.

Inexperienced travelers may think that before climbing difficult heights, it is advisable to fortify the body with meat, brandy and smoke. But these three are the greatest enemies. Our experienced Ladaki guides firmly warned us that in crossing the passes, hunger was most beneficial to men and animals, and that nothing stimulating should be taken. At each pass, we always started out before dawn, drinking but a small cup of hot tea. The horses also were given no food. The lama who was with us bled several times but the septuagenarian Chinese interpreter never had any trouble when crossing passes. Of course every superfluous movement or increased work caused weakness, giddiness and, with some people, even nausea, but a few minutes' rest restores the circulation of the blood.

We also suffered so-called mountain-blindness. Three of us had it in varying degrees—the Kalmuck, Khedub, the Tibetan, Konchok, and myself. This unpleasant trouble lasted five or six days. In my case, the right eye was affected and after two days I saw everything double, but quite clearly and distinctly. Kedub and Konchok saw everything even four times. We verified this accurately and repeatedly obtained the same results.

Equally unpleasant, especially for Mrs. Roerich, was the so-called hot snow, when the snow, reflecting the sun rays, emits an intolerable heat, from which it is impossible to find escape.

We had three other unfortunate occurrences in the caravan: attacks of heart failure which carried away three people; inflammation of the lungs, of which two more died. Several people in our caravan also suffered from scurvy and among them, one European, the chief of our transport. It must be mentioned that in Northern Tibet we met with many most severe cases of scurvy.

In addition to the main force of the Expedition, consisting of Mrs. Roerich, my son George and myself, besides the caravaneers and servants, from time to time during our long travels, we had several collaborators. During our Sikkim journey, we were accompanied by my second son, Sviatoslav and Lama Lobzang Mingyur Dorje, the well-known scholar of Tibetan literature and teacher of most of the European Tibetologists. Every traveler through Sikkim meets the cordial reception of the general of the Tibetan army, Laden-La, now in the British service, who in every way assists travelers. During our further passage, as Chinese interpreter, the septuagenarian officer of the Chinese Army, Tsai Han-chen, as well as a Kalmuck lama Lobzang, went with us. On the Altai mountains we met S. G. and M. M. Lichtmann. After Urga, the expedition was augmented by Dr. Riabinin, by the chief of our transport Porten and by two sisters, unusual helpers of Mrs. Roerich, Ludmilla and Raya Bogdanova, local Cossack girls of which the younger one, Raya, was only thirteen years old at the time they joined the expedition. I believe she was the youngest non-Tibetan that has ever crossed the severe uplands of Tibet. The presence of three women, who shared all the dangers of the terrible frosts and hardships of the way, must be definitely stressed. In Sharagolchi before Ulan-Davan, two members were added—Colonel K. and G., in charge of expedition supplies.

Let us begin with Sikkim:

This blessed country, full of reminiscences of the illumined leaders of religions, leaves an impression of great calmness. Here lived Padma Sambhava, the founder of the Red Cap sect. Atisha, who proclaimed the teaching of Kalachakra, crossed this country on his way to Tibet. Here, in the caves, dwelt many ascetics, filling the space with powerful thoughts.

Behind Kinchenjunga, in subterranean caves, still live hermits, and only a trembling hand, stretched out for food in answer to a pre-arranged knock, indicates that the physical body is still alive. All seventeen peaks of the Himalayas shine above Sikkim. From West to East, they are Kang Peak, Jannu, Little Khabru, Khabru, Dom Peak, Talung Peak, Talung saddle, Kinchenjunga, Pandim, Jubonu, Simvoo, Narsing, Siniolchu, Pakichu, Chomiomo, Lama Andem, Kanchenjhau.

It is a whole snowy realm, altering its outlines with every variation of light! Verily it is inexhaustible in impressions and incessantly evoking.

Nowhere else on earth are expressed two such entirely different worlds. Here is the earthly world, with its rich vegetation, brilliant butterflies, pheasants, leopards, panthers, monkeys, snakes and the innumerable other animals, which inhabit the ever-green jungles of Sikkim. And above the clouds, in unexpected heights, shines the snowy kingdom, which has nothing in common with the busy ant-hill of the jungles. It is an eternally moving ocean of clouds, with untold varieties of mist.

Kinchenjunga has attracted the attention equally of

Tibetans and Indians. Here was created the inspiring myth about Shiva, who drank the poison of the world for the sake of humanity. Here, from the churning of the clouds, rose the brilliant Lakshmi, for the joy of the world.

In general, a beneficent atmosphere is maintained in the monasteries of Sikkim also. On every hill, on every summit, as far as the eye can reach, you see white points—these are all strongholds of the teaching of Padma Sambhava, the official religion of Sikkim. The Maharajah of Sikkim, who lives in Gangtok, is deeply religious. The Maharanee, his wife, is of Tibetan descent and her education is quite exceptional compared to the usual Tibetan.

All monasteries of Sikkim are associated with some relics and ancient traditions. Here lived Padma Sambhava himself. Here the Teacher meditated upon a rock. When this rock splits anew, it means that the life of this place has diverted from the path of righteousness.

The Pemayangtse monastery is the official center of religion in Sikkim. Near the monastery are still seen ruins of the ancient palace of former Maharajahs. But far greater spiritual importance is attached to the old monastery Tashi-ding, which is one day's march away from Pemayangtse. Every traveler should visit this remarkable place, despite the difficult path by a bamboo bridge over a wild torrent.

We were in Tashi-ding in February, at the time of the Tibetan New Year, when thousands of visitors from the neighboring villages lend an exceptional picturesqueness to the ancient place. At that season in Tashi-ding is also performed the annual miracle of the Chalice. Every year an ancient stone chalice is half filled with water and sealed in the presence of the lamas and representatives of the Maharajah. The following year, also on New Year's day, the casket, where the chalice is kept, is unsealed. The old silk, in which the chalice is wrapped, is removed and according to the amount of water in the chalice, the future is predicted. The water either decreases, or, as is told, sometimes increases. Thus it was said to have considerably increased in 1914, before the great war, and such increase always means calamity and war.

In all monasteries of Sikkim you can feel a friendly attitude toward foreigners and the hospitable atmosphere is undisturbed. The head lamas readily show you their treasures, among which are many old objects of fine workmanship.

We were in Sikkim at the time of the third ill-fated Everest Expedition and the lamas told us: "We wonder why the pelings—foreigners—take such trouble in climbing. They will not be successful. Many of our lamas have been on the top of Mount Everest, only they were there in their astral bodies."

In these places many things, seemingly strange to the European, appear quite natural. Recently at Darjeeling, a strange episode took place with an old lama. During a disorder in the street, an old lama, a casual spectator, was arrested by the police together with the guilty agitators of the disorder. The lama did not protest and together with all the others was sentenced to a certain term of imprisonment. When the term was over and the lama was to be released, he asked permission to remain in prison, because it was quiet and most suitable for concentration!

Sikkim also accompanied us with wonderful, beneficent legends. In the temple, for instance, while the gigantic trumpets roared, the lama asked:

"Do you know why the trumpets of our temples have so resonant a tone?"

Then he explained: "The ruler of Tibet decided to summon from India, from the places where dwelt the Blessed One, a learned lama, in order to purify the fundaments of the teaching. How to meet the guest? The High Lama of Tibet, inspired by a vision, gave the design of a new trumpet so that the guest should be received with unprecedented sound; and the meeting was a wonderful one—not by the wealth of gold but by the grandeur of sound!" . . .

"And do you know why the gongs in the temple ring out with such great volume? As silver, resound the gongs and bells at dawn and evening, when the high currents are tense. Their sound reminds one of the beautiful legend of the Chinese emperor and the great lama: In order to test the knowledge and clairvoyance of the lama, the emperor made him a seat out of sacred books, and covering them with fabrics, invited the guest to sit down. The Lama said certain prayers and then sat down.

"The emperor demanded of him: 'If your knowledge

is so universal, how could you sit down on the sacred books?'

" 'There are no sacred volumes,' answered the lama. And the astonished emperor, instead of his sacred volumes, found only empty paper.

"The emperor thereupon gave to the lama many gifts and bells of liquid chime. But the lama ordered them to be thrown into the river, saying: 'I will not be able to carry these. If they are necessary to me, the river will bring these gifts to my monastery.'

"And indeed the waters carried to him the bells, with their crystal chimes, clear as the waters of the river."

About talismans, the lama also explained:

"Talismans are regarded as sacred. A mother many times asked her son to bring her a sacred relic of Buddha. But the youth forgot her request. A half day's journey from his house, he recalled his mother's request. But where can one find sacred objects in the desert? There is nought. But the traveler espied the skull of a dog. He decided to take out a tooth and, folding it in yellow silk, he brought it to the house.

"The old woman asked of him: 'Have you again forgotten my last request, my son?' He then gave her the dog's tooth wrapped in silk, saying: 'This is the tooth of Buddha.'

"And the mother put the tooth into her shrine, and performed before it the most sacred rites, directing all her worship to her holy-of-holies. And the miracle was accomplished. The tooth began to glow with a pure ray and many miracles and sacred objects resulted from it."

Even briefly I cannot refrain from mentioning evidences of will power, which occur in these places. During the visit of the Tashi Lama to India, he was asked whether it was true that he had some special psychic powers. The spiritual leader of Tibet smiled, but did not reply. But within a few minutes the Tashi Lama disappeared. All present began to search for the Tashi Lama, but in vain. Then a newcomer entered the garden where this occurred and was surprised at the unusual sight: the Tashi Lama was sitting quietly under a tree and round him, anxiously and in vain, many people were searching for him!

Or another case of will-power: In the train of the Bengal railway was found a Sadhu without a ticket. He was put off the train at the next station. The Sadhu sat on the platform, not far from the engine and remained motionless. The signal was given for the train to leave but the train did not move. The passengers, already displeased at the treatment accorded the Sadhu, paid special attention to this fact. The signal was given again—and again the train did not move. Then the passengers demanded that the Sadhu be brought back. The holy man was solemnly reinstated on his seat, and then the train was sent on safely.

* * *

I will not pause to speak of Benares, or its Sanskrit pandits, or the sacred ceremonies on the Ganges. Let us not be surprised that a great part of Sarnath, the memorial site where Buddha began his sermons, is still unexplored under earth. Even those ruins, which one may now see, have also been excavated only recently. A strange fate follows most of the places connected with the personal activity of the great founder of Buddhism. Kapilavastu and Kushinagara, the places of birth and death of the Lord Buddha, are in ruins; Sarnath is not yet completely excavated. There is some special significance in this fact. Until recently, several scientists tried to prove that Gautama Buddha never existed.

In spite of the facts in the voluminous Buddhist literature, in spite of the inscriptions on the ancient columns of King Ashoka, the French scientist Senart, in his book, has tried to prove that Buddha never existed and was nothing more than a solar myth. But here, also, our exact knowledge has provided the evidence of the human existence of Gautama Buddha. For soon after, there was excavated in Piprava, in Nepalese Terrai, the urn, dated with an inscription, containing the ashes and bones of Lord Buddha. A similar historical casket, with part of the relics of the Teacher, buried by King Kanishka, was found near Peshawar and also testifies definitely to the existence of the Great Teacher. It is curious to note that the last discovery was made in accordance with chronicles of old Chinese writers noted for the accuracy of their narratives. We had occasion to convince ourselves more than once of this.

* * *

The Northern Punjab, as for instance Harapa, north of Lahore, provides much historic material concerning the most ancient epoch of India, and also Buddhism and medieval India of the 7th century. Buddhism is not forgotten here. Gautama Rishi, as the local Punjabi and Pahari name the Lord Buddha, is greatly venerated. The ruins of ancient Buddhist temples, with typical Buddhist images, indicate that here, on the ancient road from Tibet, Buddhism flourished for ages. In the Kuluta (or Kulu) Valley alone, 363 Rishis are locally worshiped. This place in general is connected with the greatest names. It is said that Arjuna laid a subterranean passage from Kulu to Manikaran. Here also, in Mandi State, is the famous Ravalsar Lake, connected with the name of Padma Sambhava. Even now, many lamas descend into the valley from Tibet over the Shipki and Rothang passes, to worship the memory of the Teacher. The places are filled with reminiscences, for Mani and Kulu form the miraculous land, Zahor, to which such tribute is paid in Tibetan literature. The experienced scientist, Dr. A. H. Franke, in his book "Antiquities of Ancient Tibet", quotes the following:

"Let me now add a few words about Mandi, collected from Tibetan historical works. There can exist no reasonable doubt as regards the identification of the Tibetan Zahor with Mandi; for on our visit to Ravalsar we met with numerous Tibetan pilgrims, who said that they were traveling to Zahor, thereby indicating the Mandi State, if not the town. In the biography of Padma Sambhava, and in other books referring to his time, Zahor is frequently mentioned as a place where this teacher (750 A. D.) resided. The famous Buddhist teacher Santa Rakshita, who went to Tibet, was born in Zahor. Again in the days of Ral-pa-chan (800 A.D.) we find the statement that during the reigns of his ancestors many religious books had been brought to Tibet from India, Li, Zahor and Kashmir. Lahor was then apparently a seat of Buddhist learning and it is even stated that under the same king, Zahor was conquered by the Tibetans. But under his successor, the apostate King Langdarma, many religious books were brought to Zahor, among other places, to save them from destruction.

"Among the Tibetans there still prevails a tradition regarding the existence of hidden books in Mandi, and this tradition in all probability refers to the books above mentioned. Mr. Howell, Assistant Commissioner of Kulu, told me that the present Thakur of Kulong, Lahul, had once been told by a high lama from Nepal where the books are still hidden."

You see what remarkable traditions are connected with Kulu and Mandi, the ancient Kuluta and Zahor. The scientific world up to now, hopes in vain to find the most ancient copies of Buddhist books.

Not only Buddhist antiquities, not only the name of Arjuna, is connected with Kulu Valley, but even the Manu—the First Lawgiver, himself—gave his name to the village, Manali.

In Kulu valley resided Vyasa, the famous compiler of the Mahabharata. Here is Vyasakund, the sacred place of fulfilment of all wishes.

On the border of Lahul in the rocks there are two

carved images of a man and a woman about nine feet high. The same legend is told about them as about the gigantic images of Bamian in Afghanistan, that their height corresponds to that of the original inhabitants of this place.

In the same way, Kashmir is full of antiques. Here is Martand and Avantipur, connected with the flourishing of the activity of King Avantisvamin. Here are many ruins of temples and cities of the Sixth, Seventh and Eighth Centuries, in which the architectural detail surprises one by its similarity to the early Romanesque. Of the Buddhist times, almost nothing has survived in Kashmir, although here lived such pillars of the old Buddhism as Nagarjuna, Asvaghosha, Rakshita and many others, who afterwards suffered during the change from Buddhism to Hinduism. Here is the "Throne of Solomon" and on the same summit, the foundation of the temple laid by the son of King Ashoka. I will not speak of Srinagar itself. True, in the rough laying of the quay stones of the river, and the foundations of the building, one can trace singular stones with beautiful carving, belonging to the best time. But these are partial fragments, which have nothing in common with the present sad position of the city.

In Srinagar we first encountered the curious legend about Christ's visit to this place. Afterwards we saw how widely spread in India, in Ladak and in Central Asia, was the legend of the visit of Christ to these parts during his long absence, quoted in the Gospel. The Moslems of Srinagar told us that the crucified Christ—or, as they call Him, Issa—did not die on the cross, but only lost consciousness. The disciples took away His body, secreted it and cured Him. Later, Issa was taken to Srinagar, where He taught the people. And there He died. The tomb of the Teacher is in the basement of a private house. It is said that an inscription exists there stating that the son of Joseph was buried there. Near the tomb, miraculous cures are said to take place and fragrant aromas to fill the air. In this way, the people of other religions desire to have Christ among them.

* * *

The ancient caravan road from Srinagar to Leh is covered in a seventeen days' march. But it is usually advised to take a few days more. Only cases of extreme need can induce the traveler to make this journey without interruption. Such unforgettable places, as Maulbeck, Lamayuru, Basgu, Kharbu, Saspul, Spithug, arrest one and retain themselves forever in one's memory, both from an artistic and a historical point of view.

Maulbeck—now already a declining monastery, to judge by the ruins—must have once been a real stronghold, boldly occupying the summit of a huge rock. Near Maulbeck, on the main road, you are startled by an ancient gigantic image of Maitreya. You feel that not a Tibetan hand, but probably a Hindu, carved this image at the time of Buddhist glory.

Fa-hsien, the Chinese traveler, in his chronicles, mentions a huge image of Maitreya here. We wonder whether his mention refers to this relief. When we were already approaching Khotan we heard, quite by chance, that at the back of this rock is an ancient Chinese inscription. In this place we might have expected a Sanskrit, Tibetan and even a Mongolian inscription, but Chinese is quite a surprise. Let the next explorer study the back of the rock of Maitreya. Further on the way, you become accustomed to these gigantic monuments and structures which, like eagles, hold in their grip these high waterless summits. But the first impression, as usual, is the most striking.

One must have a sense of beauty and of fearless self denial to build strongholds on such heights. In many such castles, long subterranean passages, leading to a river, were hewn in the rocks, so that a loaded donkey could just manage to pass there. This fairy-tale of subterranean passages, as we shall see, has created many of the best sagas. As in Sikkim, the Ladaki lamas turned out to be kind, tolerant of other faiths and hospitable to travelers, as Buddhists should be.

All three of the main teachings of Lamaism can be found in Ladak: Gelukpa—the yellow faith, proclaimed by Tsong-kha-pa. The Red cap sect, the followers of Padma Sambhava, and even the oldest Bon-po, the so-called Black faith, of pre-Buddhist origin. These worshippers of the gods of Svastika still remain for us an inexplicable enigma. From one side they are sorcerers, Shamans, perverters of Buddhism. But, on the other hand, in their teaching can be found faint traces of Druidic fire and nature worship. The literature of

Bon-po has not yet been translated, is not interpreted and deserves, in any case, thorough research.

With even more interest we approached Lamayuru. This monastery is considered a stronghold of Bon-po. Of course, the Bon-po of Lamayuru is not a true Bon-po. It is already considerably mixed with Lamaism and Buddhism. In the monastery there is an image of Buddha and also one of Maitreya. This is of course quite incompatible with the basic principles of the black faith. But the monastery itself and its situation is quite unique in its fairy-like beauty. We thought to ourselves, that if we encountered such beautiful sights in Ladak (Little Tibet), then what could we not expect in Tibet!

An equally romantic impression of majesty is conveyed by Basgu, where the present-day temples are intermingled with ancient ruins. These ruins are attributed to Zorawar and other Kashmir conquerors, who invaded Ladak, mercilessly destroying Buddhist monasteries. All these half-ruined towers and endlessly long walls, crowning the peaks of rocks, speak of the ancient glory of Ladak and of the valiant spirit of its founders. The name of the great hero of Asia—Gessar Khan—rings over these places.

In Kalatse, near the old fort, on a shaky bridge across the yellow thundering Indus, you hear the story of how the hand of Sukamir, the Kashmir invader, defeated by the Ladaki, was nailed to the bridge as a sign of warning. "But", adds the story-teller, "a cat ate the hostile hand, and in order to keep up the moral lesson, the hand of a dead lama had to be nailed to the bridge." Such is the play of fate.

In Saspul we again find a remarkable temple with most ancient images of Maitreya. The literature of Ladak is extensive. But one feels that still more may be discovered here, restoring the lost milestones of many an ancient path.

On the rocks, half-way up to Kashmir, some ancient carvings may be seen. They are regarded as Dard images and are ascribed to the ancient inhabitants of Dardistan. On more closely studying these typical carvings on the surfaces of the rocks, one may distinguish two different types: One is new, drier in its technique. On them one may see suggestions of Buddhist objects, stylizations of suburgans and so-called fortunate signs of Buddhism. But near them, sometimes on the same rocks, one may see a rich soft technique, reminding one of Neoliths. In these ancient images one may distinguish ibexes with huge, powerfully curved horns, yaks, hunters, archers, round dancers and rituals. The character of these carvings merits careful attention, because one may find similar designs on the rocks near the oasis Sanju in Sinkiang, in Siberia, in the Trans-Himalayas, and one remembers them in the Halristningar of Scandinavia. Let us not hurry with conclusions, but let us study and compare.

In Nimu, a small village before Leh, 11,000 feet high, we had an experience which can under no circumstances be overlooked. It would be most interesting to hear of analogous cases. It was after a clear, calm day. We camped in tents. At about 10 p. m. I was already asleep, when Mrs. Roerich approached her bed to remove the woolen rug. But hardly had she touched the wool, when a big rose-violet flame of the color of an intense electric discharge shot up, forming a seemingly whole bonfire, about a foot high. A shout of Mrs. Roerich, "Fire, fire!" awoke me. Jumping up, I saw the dark silhouette of Mrs. Roerich and behind her, a moving flame, clearly illuminating the tent. Mrs. Roerich tried to extinguish the flame with her hands, but the fire flashed through her fingers, escaping her hands, and burst into several smaller fires. The effect of the touch was a slightly warming effect, but there was no burning, nor sound, nor odor. Gradually the flames diminished and finally disappeared, leaving no traces whatsoever on the bed cover. We had occasion to study many electric phenomena, but I must say that we never experienced one of such proportions.

In Darjeeling, a spheroidic lightning passed only two feet from my head. In Gulmarg, in Kashmir, during an uninterrupted thunderstorm of three days, when hail fell as big as a pigeon's egg, we studied a great variety of lightning. In the Trans-Himalayas, we repeatedly experienced the effect upon ourselves of different electric phenomena. I remember how in Chunargen, at an altitude of 15,000 feet, I awoke at night in my tent, and touching my bedrug, was surprised at the blue light flashing from my fingertips as though enwrapping my hand. Believing that this could occur only in contact with woolen material, I touched the linen pillowcase.

The effect was again the same. Then I touched all kinds of objects—wood, paper, canvas; in each case the blue light flashed up, intangible, soundless and odorless.

The entire Himalayan region offers exceptional fields for scientific research. Nowhere else, in the whole world, can such varied conditions be concentrated: peaks up to almost thirty thousand feet; lakes at an elevation of fifteen thousand feet; deep valleys with geysers and all types of hot and cold mineral springs; the most unsuspected vegetation—all this vouches for unprecedented results in new scientific discoveries. If one could compare scientifically the conditions of the Himalayas with the uplands of other parts of the world, what remarkable analogies and antitheses would arise! The Himalayas are a veritable Mecca for a sincere scientist. When we recalled the book of Professor Millikan, "The Cosmic Ray", we imagined the wonderful possibilities which this great scientist would find on these Himalayan heights. May these dreams become true, in the name of true science!

The city of Leh, the residence of the former Maharajah of Ladak, now conquered by Kashmir, is a typical Tibetan town, with numerous clay walls, temples and long rows of Suburgans, which lend a solemn silence to the place. This city, on a high mountain, is crowned by the eight-story palace of the Maharajah. At the latter's invitation, we stopped there, choosing for our dwelling the top floor of the stronghold, which trembled under the violent gusts of wind. During our occupancy a door and part of the wall collapsed. But the wonderful view from the roof made us forget the instability of the castle.

Below the palace, lies the whole city: bazaars crowded with noisy caravans, fruit orchards and, around the city, great fields of barley from which garlands of merry songs resound at the close of the day's work. The Ladaki women walk about picturesquely in their high fur caps, with turned up ear-pieces. Down their backs hang long head-bands decorated with a great amount of turquoise and small metal ornaments. Across the shoulders, like an ancient Byzantine korsno, is generally worn the skin of a yak, fastened on the right shoulder with a fibula. Among the richer women, this korsno is of colored cloth, resembling still more the real Byzantine ikons. And the fibulae on their right shoulder might have been excavated in Nordic and Scandinavian tumuli.

Not far from Leh, on a stony hill, are ancient graves, believed to be prehistoric and recalling Druidic antiquities. Not far away is also the place of the old Mongolian Kham, which tried to conquer Ladak. In this valley also are Nestorian crosses, once more recalling how widely spread in Asia was Nestorianism and Manicheism.

In Leh, we again encountered the legend of Christ's visit to these parts. The Hindu postmaster of Leh, and several Ladaki Buddhists told us that in Leh not far from the bazaar, there still exists a pond, near which stood an old tree. Under this tree, Christ preached to the people, before his departure to Palestine. We also heard another legend of how Christ, when young, arrived in India with a merchant's caravan and how He continued to study the higher wisdom in the Himalayas. We heard several versions of this legend which has spread widely throughout Ladak, Sinkiang and Mongolia, but all versions agree on one point, that during the time of His absence, Christ was in India and Asia. It does not matter how and from where the legend originated. Perhaps it is of Nestorian origin. It is valuable to see that the legend is told in full sincerity.

The entire atmosphere at Ladak seemed to be under benevolent signs for us.

We gathered our caravan to cross to Khotan over the Karakorum pass, without much difficulty. Two roads were possible, one over seven passes, and the other, along the River Shayok, with less passes, but with a long stretch in water. The men of the caravan preferred the first route over the mountain passes, rather than to wade through the fairly deep Shayok in September and risk catching cold.

So we left Leh on the 19th of September. And it was high time, for the monsoon of Kashmir, turning into snowy clouds, drove us northward.

* * *

As we left the town, the local women met us on the road, carrying consecrated yak's milk, with which they anointed the foreheads of people and animals, wishing us a happy journey. And they had cause, for the mountain passes can be most severe. Afterwards, in Khotan, we saw people who had been carried down from the passes with their limbs frozen black, and we heard how a year ago near Khardong a whole caravan, with about a hundred horses, was found frozen. Men were found standing up, seemingly alive, some of them with their hands to their mouths, apparently uttering their last cry. And, indeed, on the heights, on frosty mornings, the limbs and hands freeze very quickly. The Ladaki now and then, solicitously ran up to us, offering to rub our feet and hands.

Of the seven passes of this road—Khardong, Karaul Davan, Sasser, Dapsang, Karakorum, Suget and Sanju —Sasser turned out to be most dangerous, especially the rising of the glacier slope, smooth and spherical, where George's horse slipped.

The last pass, Sanju, is also most unpleasant, because here one has to jump over a pretty wide crevice. One should not touch the reins, but give the experienced hill yak his own way.

The Suget Pass, quite unexpectedly, afforded us an unpleasant experience. The ascent from its southern side, is quite easy. But a terrible snow storm arose and, approaching the descending slope, we saw that the narrow zig-zagged path was completely obstructed by snow. Near the precipice four caravans had collected, comprising about 400 horses and mules. A party of very experienced old mules was sent down ahead without riders and the careful animals, struggling through the deep snow, felt their way along the narrow path. Then the other caravans followed, stumbling and slipping.

Of all the seven passes, Karakorum turned out to be the easiest, although the highest. Karakorum means

"Black Throne" and is called so because of the black rock which crowns the crest.

To describe the beauty of this snowy realm, where we spent many days, is quite impossible. Such variations, such expressiveness of outline, such fantastic cities, such multicolored streams and torrents, and such memorable purple and moon-like cliffs!

And at the same time one feels the astounding silence of the desert! People stop their disputes, all differences disappear, and all, without exception, sense the beauty of these no-man's heights. On the way, we encountered touching caravan traditions. Often we saw bales of goods, left behind, unguarded, by unknown owners. Perhaps the animals fell or became too fatigued to carry the goods, which were left for another occasion. And nobody would touch this property. Nobody would dare to transgress this ethic of the caravan. We smiled, imagining what would happen if one left unguarded property in a city street. Yes, in the desert one enjoys greater safety.

Nobody knows exactly where is the frontier between Ladak and Chinese Turkestan. It is there, somewhere between Karakorum and Kurul! In Kurul is the first Chinese outpost. It is as if nobody owned the beautiful desert! As if it was an unknown land! There are even few animals there. We also met only a few caravans. Among them were Moslem pilgrims bound for Mecca, with their wares, to earn a green turban and the honorable surname of "Haji".

Caravans meet on most friendly terms by night. They

help each other with their smaller needs and over the red campfires ten fingers are raised in lively narrations of unusual events. The most dissimilar and varied people meet in this way: Ladaki, Kashmiris, Afghans, Tibetans, Astoris, Baltis, Dards, Mongols, Sarts, Chinese, and every one has his own tale, nurtured in the silence of the desert.

Kurul is the first Chinese outpost on the Yarungkash-darya, the river of black nephrite. It forms a square, bound by dented clay walls. Inside is a dirty yard with small clay buildings, leaning against the wall of the fort. In a tiny clay hut lives the Chinese officer. On the wall hangs a long single-barreled gun with a large single cock. This constitutes the entire arms of the officer. With him are a Kirghiz interpreter and about twenty-five men from the Kirghiz militia. The officer himself turns out to be a Chinese of good type. He examines our Chinese passport, issued by the Chinese Ambassador in Paris, Cheng-Lo, by order of the Chinese Government. Our old Chinese thoughtfully repeats: "Chinese soil". Is he pleased or sorrowful about something?

From Kurul one may go either by a round-about route through Kok-yar, or across the last pass, Sanju, to Sanju Oasis and Khotan. We chose the more difficult but shorter way. On approaching the Sanju pass itself, we found Buddhist caves which have not been described heretofore and which the local inhabitants call "Kirghiz dwellings." The approach to the caves was obstructed by land slides and we looked up longingly to the high dark openings, cut off from the road. There are perhaps frescoes and other antiques.

Near Sanju Oasis, the hills become smaller, and finally change into a sandy desert. Whoever has seen Egypt, will understand the character of this land with its rosy reflections. On the last rock we saw a neolithic design of the same ibexes and daring archers, which we saw in Ladak. And in front of us, was the rosy mist of Taklamakan and the welcoming dastarkhan of the elders of the local Sarts. On the next day, already behind the Sanju Oasis, we noticed in the very desert itself, a solitary rider approaching. He stopped, gazed sharply around, dismounted and set something on the ground. Approaching, we saw a white cloth, and on it a pumpkin and two pomegranates. A truly enchanted table: the greeting of an unknown friend.

We moved along barkhans of quicksand, often without trace of a road, and it was difficult to imagine that we were on the great Chinese Imperial highway, the so-called silk road, the main western artery of old China. The picturesque mazars, the burial sites of the hill Kirghiz, ended and the mosques of the Sarts began, simple and plain as the clay houses of Sarts, gathered in small oases amid the threatening sands.

When we were in the open sands, three doves came flying up to the caravan and continued flying before us, as though calling us somewhere. One of the local men smiled and said: "You see, the sacred bird is calling you. You must visit the old mazar, guarded by the doves."

So we turned from the road, and went to the old mazar and mosque, around which thousands of pigeons hovered, protected by the legend that he who dares to kill one of these birds, perishes immediately. According to tradition, we bought grain for the birds, and continued our travels.

It was the tenth of October, but the sun was still so hot, that the stirrups burned the foot through the boots.

* * *

A day's march from Khotan, grass began to appear on the sandy barkhans, and the clay houses became more numerous. We entered the Khotan oasis, a region which Fa-hsien in 400 A. D. described as follows:

"The land is rich and happy. The people prosper. They are all Buddhists. Their greatest recreation is religious music. There are several thousand priests and they belong to the Mahayana. They all receive food from the communal food-stores." Of course, present-day Khotan does not correspond in the slightest to the description of Fa-hsien. Long dirty bazaars and demolished clay houses do not convey the impression of wealth and prosperity. Of course, there is no evidence of Buddhism either. The few Chinese temples are very rarely open and the Confucian gongs did not sound once during the entire four-months' period of our involuntary stay there.

Of 150,000 Sarts, there are but a few hundred Chinese, and the masters of the land have become the guests. Old Khotan was about six miles away, where the village Yotkan, stands to-day. The old Buddhist sites have now been covered by mosques, mazars and Moslem dwellings, so that further excavations in these places are quite out of question.

Khotan itself is at present in a transitory state. It had already turned away from the old. The high quality and finesse of the old workmanship has disappeared, although they have not overtaken contemporary civilization. Everything is without form, unstable, and somehow transitory. The jade carvings are coarse. The Buddhist antiques, which up to recently were brought to Khotan from the neighborhood, have almost all disappeared. But to our surprise, we saw many imitations, which were sometimes very accurately made and showed taste. All antiquities from Khotan should be well examined. In Khotan we also saw imitations of rugs, very well made, copying the editions of the British Museum. If these rugs are called imitations, it is quite all right; but if they follow customary procedure and pass into the hands of antique dealers, this would be very unfortunate. In its essence, Khotan still remains a rich oasis. The loess of the soil is very fertile, and the yield of grain and fruit is abundant.

Permit these places at least the elementary conditions of culture, and prosperity may be restored at once. The people are very sympathetic, but in this large oasis, with over 200,000 inhabitants, there is no hospital, no doctor, no dentist. We have seen people perishing from the most hideous diseases, without any help whatsoever. The nearest assistance, also only a voluntary one, is the

Swedish Mission in Yarkend, an entire week's journey from Khotan.

One must say that the present rulers of China care very little, if at all, to attract useful cultural elements to these parts.

While approaching Khotan, we heard the story of how a year ago the Khotan Tao-tai Ma, acting on the orders of the governor-general of Sinkiang, Yang-Tutu, crucified and then murdered the old Titai of Kashgar. On the way people told us: "Better do not go to Khotan, the Tao-tai there is a bad man." Their warnings afterwards turned out to be prophetic.

After the first friendly official meeting, the Tao-tai and Amban of Khotan informed us, that they did not recognize the passports issued by order of the Peking Government and that they could not permit us to leave Khotan; they seized our arms, prohibited scientific work of any kind, and also forbade our painting. It appeared that the Tao-tai and Amban could not distinguish a plan from a painting. I will not lose time over these unpleasantnesses which proved the stupidity of the Tao-tai. I will only mention that, instead of the short stay as we intended, we were detained in Khotan for four months and only at the end of January, thanks to the assistance of the British Consul in Kashgar, Major Gillan, could we continue our journey to Yarkend, Kashgar, Kuchar, Karashahr and Urumchi. The journey took seventy-four days.

The first part of the journey was along the snow-covered desert, but in Yarkend, at the beginning of

February, the last patches of snow disappeared, and again there rose clouds of choking sand dust. But we were happy on the other hand to see the first leaves of the fruit trees. The Amban of Yarkend was a man of far greater education than the Khotan authorities. He expressed his deep indignation at the absurd actions of Khotan, and approved of our passports, which, he said, were the usual ones, according to which he had to assist us in every possible manner. In Yarkend, in Yangihissar and in Kashgar, we met the friendly aid of Swedish missionaries, who supplied us with much information about the extraordinary fertility of the region and about the colossal mineral wealth, which lies absolutely untouched.

Kashgar, with its triple walls and sand cliffs, along the high river bed, gives the impression of a typical Asiatic town. Both the Chinese Tao-tai and the British consul there met us heartily. And again everything unrecognized in Khotan, was accepted as fully valid. Even our arms were returned to us, that is, we were permitted to carry them ourselves, in a closed box, to the governor-general in Urumchi. Incidentally, during our entire journey to Urumchi, we had not one occasion to regret that our arms were sealed.

In Kashgar it was most instructive to visit what was apparently the oldest part of the city, on the opposite shore of the river, where a considerable part of an old Stupa may still be seen. This Stupa is about as large as the great Stupa of Sarnath. Below Kashgar, are several ancient Buddhist caves, which have already been explored and which are connected with poetic legends. About six miles from Kashgar is the Miriam Mazar, the so-called tomb of the Holy Virgin, Mother of Christ. The legend relates that, after the persecution of Jesus in Jerusalem, Miriam fled to Kashgar, where the place of her burial is marked by a mazar, worshipped up till today.

From Kashgar to Aksu the road is most tedious, partly due to the all-penetrating dust, and also to the deep quicksands and lifeless forests of gnarled desert poplars, half-burnt. It is the custom of travelers to set a tree on fire, instead of building a camp fire.

In Aksu, we met the first Chinese Amban to speak English. The young man dreamt of escaping from that sandy place as soon as possible. He showed us a Shanghai English newspaper, which he had received from Mr. Cavaliere, the postmaster in Urumchi, an Italian. I was surprised that the Amban did not subscribe to a newspaper himself, but later discovered that the all-powerful Yang-tutu had prohibited his subjects from reading newspapers. Later on we shall see the somewhat original methods which this ruler of all Sinkiang adopted in governing his country.

The neighborhood of Kuchar is full of the ancient Buddhist cave temples, which provided so many of the beautiful monuments of Central Asiatic art. This art, with full merit, has received a high place among the monuments of ancient cultures. But despite the attention accorded to this art, it seems to me that it has not yet been fully valued, especially from the point of artistic composition.

The site of the former cave-monastery, close to Kuchar, makes an unforgettable impression. In a gorge, rows of different caves are set like an amphitheatre, all decorated with mural paintings and showing traces of many statues, which have either been destroyed or removed. One may well imagine the solemnity of this place at the time when the kingdom of the Tokhars was at its height. The mural painting has partly remained.

One often has cause to resent the actions of European explorers, who have removed whole parts of architectural ensembles to museums. One can sanction the removal of separate objects which have already lost their identity with any definite monument. But is it not unjust, from the local stand-point, to hack apart arbitrarily a composition which still stands? Would it not be a pity to cut in pieces Tuanhuang, the best preserved of the monuments of Central Asia? We do not dismember Italian frescoes. Of course, there is this consideration: The majority of Buddhist monuments on Moslem lands have been and still are, exposed to iconoclastic fanaticism. In order to destroy the images, fires are built in the caves, and as high as the hand can reach, the faces of the images have been scratched with knives. We have seen traces of such destruction. The labors of such distinguished scholars as Sir Aurel Stein, Pelliot, Le Coq, Oldenburg, have safeguarded many of the monuments, which otherwise would have suffered the greatest danger of destruction, because of the carelessness of the Chinese administration.

The old Central Asiatic artist, besides his knowledge of valuable iconographic details, showed a highly developed decorative feeling and great ability to combine wealth of detail with general composition, in covering large surfaces. You can well imagine, how many impressions one may gather, when each day one makes additional observations, and when the generosity of antiquity, together with nature, provides inexhaustible artistic material.

Kuchar is a large city, entirely Moslem, and there is nothing to recall the departed kingdom of the Tokhars with its highly developed literature and education. It is said that the last Uigur king, when threatened by his enemies, fled from Kuchar, carrying with him all his treasures. Perceiving the endless, winding mountain ridges, one may imagine that there is enough room for these treasures to be hidden. In any case, the old treasures of this land have gone. But the richly laden fruit trees convince one that with but slight efforts, new treasures could easily be accumulated again.

On the entire journey from Kuchar to Karashahr, we were accompanied by Buddhist memories. On the left of the road, there appeared, as though in faint mist, the mountain branches of the magnificent T'ien-Shan, the heavenly mountains. Someone appreciated their ethereal blue tone and named them fittingly. In these hills already can be found the permanent and nomadic monasteries of the Kalmucks. Karashahr, Olut and

Khoshut horsemen are seen instead of Sart Moslem towns.

On the way, riders approached us, already on Kalmyck saddles, and began a conversation with George and our lamas. Up till now the Kalmucks consider themselves independent and relate the following tale of how they retained their independence, during the time of the last Khan. They say:

"The Chinese set evil charms upon the late Khan and he transferred to the Chinese official the sovereignty over his people. The official hurried to Urumchi to report his success to Yang-Tutu. But the Kalmuck elders came to know of it and sent horsemen in pursuit of the Chinese caravan, overtaking it in the T'ien-Shan mountain passes. It came to pass that no one ever again heard of this caravan and no trace of it was ever discovered. The old Khan was surrounded by the elders and died soon, and Toin Lama took over the reign, because the prince was not yet of age."

Of course, the Kalmuck "independence" is only apparent to themselves. Actually, they are under the thumb of the Yang-Tutu, and their last cavalry detachment, formed by the Toin Lama, has even been removed to Urumchi. And even the Toin Lama himself became a voluntary or involuntary guest of Urumchi.

The Kalmuck steppes with their high grass, the golden-canopied yurtas of nomad monasteries, the purely Scythian garb of the riders, all make a distinct differentiation between the Sarts and Chinese of Sinkiang and the entirely individual habits of the Kalmucks.

For a time we turned aside from the T'ien-Shan, and plunged into the suffocating air of Toksun, the Turfan region. We encountered scorpions, tarantulas, subterranean canals—arycks—and an unbearable heat, during which even the local people cannot walk more than two miles. Besides remarkable monuments, besides the Mother of the World, these places provided us with many legends and a tradition of travel: It is customary in Turfan to send the young people to travel under the leadership of experienced men, for the Turfans say "travels mean victory over life."

In Karashahr and in Toksun, we noticed beautiful types of horses of the Karashahr breed. Whoever recalls the ancient Chinese terra-cottas of horses from the T'ang epoch, should not imagine that this breed has disappeared. The Karashahr horses especially recall these. Most interesting are the horses with zebra-like stripes; perhaps this breed was once crossed with wild khulans.

Urumchi is the capital of Sinkiang. Here lives the terrifying Yang-Tutu, who for seventeen years, despite all changes, rules over all Chinese Turkestan with its variety of inhabitants. The governmental methods employed by Yang-Tutu should be remembered as one of the curiosities of history. Yang-Tutu considers himself an educated man and has the degree of Magister. He constantly faces the contradictory interests of the Chinese, Sarts, Kirghiz, Kalmucks, Mongols. Sometimes the ruler proclaims himself a friend of the Kalmucks, circulating the news that the Tashi-Lama, who is in China, has been elected Emperor of China. Having won the sympathy of the Buddhists, Yang-Tutu goes over to the side of the Chinese Dungans, even stipulating in his will, to be buried in the Dungan cemetery.

In case of an insoluble racial dispute, he proclaims his inability to decide to whom to accord his sympathy, and he then stages a cock-fight to decide the matter. For this purpose, Yang-Tutu keeps several cocks of different colors. The ruler knows their qualities, and on the day of the fight, he personally chooses which of the cocks is to represent the opposing sides. The black cock may be the Dungan; the white, a Sart; a yellow cock, a Kalmuck. Thus, according to Tutu's wish, the favored nationality wins through the seeming valor of the cock. Then the ruler, raising his eyes to heaven, proclaims that his heart is open to all, but that destiny has awarded preference to the Sarts or Dungans, as is need, at the moment.

During our stay the "Magister of Philosophy" punished a god for the continuous drought. The god of water and rain was flogged. But since he still persisted in withholding rain, his hands and feet were cut off and he was drowned in the river. And in his place, a local "devil" was solemnly installed. The numerous methods of execution are apparently familiar to the "Magister of Philosophy". He generously applies them to personal enemies and disobedient officials. In Octave Mirbeau's "Garden of Torture", two subtle inventions were omitted: one is the insertion of a horse hair in the eye ball, with which the nerve is sawn through. Or a disobedient official is sent on a mission and on his way, faithful men of Yang-Tutu overtake him and plaster his face with Chinese paper, until he meets his eternal rest. Stories are related of how the murders of undesirable statesmen were cleverly staged. For some reason, these usually occurred after a generous dinner, when the executioner appeared behind the victim and unexpectedly cut off his head. In Imperial times, it was also customary to inform the victim first of the award of a new title to him!

* * *

In the streets of Urumchi, with loud drum-beats and with innumerable bright banners, marches a ragged crowd, which under your very vision disperses, disappearing in the narrow alleys: this is the army of Yang-Tutu. The army is estimated by the number of caps, and for this reason one often sees two-wheeled carts, with poles on which are hanging numerous soldiers' caps. This is the invisible army! And Yang-Tutu, drawing the pay for the number of caps enlisted, sends large quantities of silver to distant banks through foreign representatives, by means of cunning manipulations. Incidentally the ruler had no opportunity to use his wealth, as he was killed by Fan, the commissioner of foreign affairs, in 1928. It was strange in our day to see these medieval customs with the terror of torture and deep superstition. New China must send specially educated men to its provinces.

And another condition greatly astonished us in Sinkiang. I refer to the open trade in human beings—

children and adults. Already in Khotan it was seriously proposed to us not to hire servants, but to buy men and maids for good, as we were assured that this was much easier and much more economical. A good maid costs 25 sars, which is less than $20. A sais may be bought for 30 sars. Children are quite cheap—two to five sars. In Toksun, a Cossack woman from Semipalatinsk, who had married a Chinese, showed us a little Kirghiz girl, whom she bought for three sars. This was a fortunate case for the girl, because the childless woman had bought the girl as a daughter. But in general, you hear of terrible cases here and there. Insufficient attention is paid to this sad fact, as well as to the destructive habit of opium smoking. Distributors and addicts of this scourge should be subject to most severe penalty, if their consciences are so deadened that they cannot realize the crime they commit both towards themselves and towards the future generations.

But let us not leave Chinese Turkestan with these dark impressions. Before me rise four pictures recalling ancient times:

A horseman rides along and on his hand, as ages ago, sits a falcon or a trained hawk, with a small cap over its eyes.

In the desert we were overtaken by a traveling minstrel—a teller of legends and fairy tales—a Baksha. Over his shoulder hangs a long sitarah, and in his saddle bags are several varied drums. "Baksha, sing us something!"—and the traveling singer, loosening the reins of his horse, sends out into the silence of the desert, a song of Shabistan, of its beautiful princes and good and evil witches.

And another small, but significant episode: Between Aksu and Kuchar, near the town of Bai, a peculiar looking individual in shackles asked to join our caravan. It appeared that the local authorities had given orders to send the criminal with our caravan. We forbade such an addition. The criminal slackened his pace and remained in the rear. But for many days, we could see him following the caravan far behind, without any guard.

About four miles out of Urumchi, a Chinese mafa overtook us. It appeared that the Chinaman, Sung, who had been in our service as far as Khotan, could not let us go without at least another farewell. Before our departure he had wept for several nights, because the governor had forbidden him to accompany us beyond Urumchi. And the kind heart could not resist the desire to see us once more. It is always pleasant to remember such people.

* * *

Beyond Urumchi there comes a strip of land, interesting not only from an artistic, but also from a scientific and ethnographic point of view. Here we touch a region, with remnants of the great migrations of nations, such as kurgans and different burial places and stone images. On the other hand, these ranges of the Tarbagatai mountains, especially since the revolution, are infested with robbers. The Kirghiz, whose lands begin here, although outwardly resembling the Scythians and seeming like silhouettes from the vases of Kul-oba, are of little use in present day civilization. Their habitual robbing, "baranta", makes culture rather difficult. Besides, there is plenty of gold in the region of the black Irtysh and hence wandering masses of prospectors have invaded the place, and it is better not to sit round one campfire with them.

One is again surprised at the fertility of the country and how little it has been studied and exploited.

Altai or, as it is now called, Oirotiya, is equally concealed and neglected. The Oirots are a Finno-Turki tribe, at a very low state of evolution. Their outworn kaftans of sheepskin and their unkempt hair compared with some of the Tibetans. The Old Believers, who settled long ago in this remote country, are of course, the only strong masters of the place. It was pleasant to see, that the Old Believers have considerably advanced, rejecting many of their old religious prejudices. They now think correctly of domestic affairs, of American machines, and they welcome foreigners, although this was not previously the case.

Of course, the old way of living, with its picturesquely carved wooden houses, with brocaded sarafans and old ikons, has also disappeared. We wished that in the new forms of life, antiquity should not give way to the mediocrity of the bazars. For in Siberia, where there is such mineral wealth and other natural treasures, the people have the heritage of highly artistic Siberian antiques, the heritage of Yermak and fearless pioneers. When we passed the place on the Irtysh, where Yermak—the hero of Siberia—was drowned, an Altayan said to us:

"Never would our Yermak have drowned, if it were not for the heavy armour, which dragged him to the bottom!"

Meeting the Old Believers in the Altai, it was astonishing to hear of the numerous religious sects, which exist there even now.

The Popovtsy, the Bezpopovtsy, the Striguny, the Pryguni, the Pomortsi, the Netovtse (not recognizing any of the beliefs, but considering themselves of "the old faith")—how many incomprehensible discussions they occasion! And toward Trans-Baikal among the Semeiski (Old Believers exiled to Siberia with their entire families), also are added the Temnovertsy and the Kalashniki. Each of the Temnovertsy has his own ikon, closed with little doors, to which he alone prays. If anyone else should pray to the same ikon, it would become unfit! Still stranger are the Kalashniki. They pray before the ikon through a little opening in *kalach* (a loaf of bread). We have heard much, but such obscure beliefs we have never seen nor heard of—and that in the summer of 1926! Here are also Hlysty, Pashkovtsy, Stundisty and Molokans—a great variety of different beliefs, which entirely exclude each other.

But even in these forsaken corners a new conception already begins to stir and the long-bearded Old Believer speaks with enthusiasm of agricultural machinery and compares the quality of manufactures of various countries. Although the beliefs have not yet been quite obliterated, in any case the prejudice against innovations has already evaporated and sound domestic principles have not diminished, but have encouraged new sprouts. This new building up of agricultural methods, the untouched riches, the great radio-activity there, the abundance of its grass (which is higher than a man on horseback), its streams, inviting electrification—all this gives to Altai an unforgettable meaning.

In the region of Altai one can also hear many significant legends connected with vague reminiscences of tribes that passed here long ago. Among these incomprehensible tribes, are mentioned the "Blacksmiths of Kurumchi". The name indicates these people as fine metal workers, but whence did they come and whither did they go? Perhaps the popular memory alludes to the creators of the metal objects, for which the antiquities of Minusinsk and Ural are so famous? When you hear of these blacksmiths, you involuntarily recall the legendary Nibelungen, who drifted far to the west.

In this melting pot of nations, it is most instructive to observe how sometimes under your very eyes, a language may be changed. In Mongolia, we heard of the most curious combinations of expressions, made up only recently from many languages. Chinese, Mongolian, Buriat, Russian and slightly modified foreign technical words, already afford quite a new conglomeration. A new problem will arise for philologists from this creation of new expressions and even entirely new local dialects.

Altai played a most important part in the migration

of nations. The burial places of huge rocks—the so-called graves of Chud—as well as the inscriptions on rocks, all bring us back to the important epoch, when from the far south-east, impelled by glaciers, or at times by sands, nations collected themselves as an avalanche to over-run and regenerate Europe. From the prehistoric and historic point of view, Altai is an untouched treasure, and the ruler of the Altai, snow-white Beluha, who nurtures all rivers and fields, is ready to yield her treasures.

* * *

If it was important to become acquainted with the Oirots and Old Believers, then it was still more important to see the Mongols on whom at present, with justification, the world turns its eye.

It is the same Mongolia, whose very name impelled the inhabitants of the ancient Turkestan towns to flee their houses in terror, leaving behind an inscription: "God save us from the Mongols." And because of them, even fishermen in far-away Denmark feared to venture into the open sea. Thus was the world awed by the name of the terrible conquerors.

When hearing the stories about the Mongols, one is astonished by their irreconcilable contradictions. On one hand you hear, that the Mongolian army chiefs even now, on capturing an enemy, cut out his heart and eat it. And one commander even stated that if you cut out the heart of a Chinese, he only grits his teeth, but the Russians scream terribly. There are also tales of Shaman conjurers, and of how, in the darkness of the yurtas of the Shamans, you can hear the trampling of whole droves of horses, the sound of coveys of eagles in flight and the hissing of innumerable snakes. At the will of the Shaman, snow falls inside the yurta. Such manifestations of will power indeed exist. Incidentally, is it not possible that the word "Shaman" is a depraved form of the Sanskrit "Shraman", just as "Bokhara" is nothing but the altered Buddhist word "Vihara"?

In Urga they related to us the following episode, showing the will power of certain lamas: a certain man received word from a revered lama that after two years of prosperity, great danger would befall him, if he would remain in Urga after a given date. Two years passed in full prosperity, and as is often the case, the successful man entirely forgot the warning. Unexpectedly, the revolution broke out and the opportunity to leave Urga safely was missed. Terrified, the man hurried to the lama again. The latter, reproving him, promised to save him once again and ordered him to depart the next morning with his whole family. "But", he added, "should you meet soldiers, do not try to run away, but remain absolutely motionless." The man did as the lama told him. On the way a detachment of soldiers approached. The family stopped and remained silent and motionless. As the soldiers passed near them, they heard one of them say to another:

"Look, what's that? People?"

But the other man replied: "What's the matter? Are you blind? Can't you see they are stones!"

When you visit the Mongolian printing press in Urga and speak to the Minister of Education, Batukhan, and to the well-known Buriato-Mongolian scholar, honorary secretary of the Scientific Committee, Djemsarano: when you become acquainted with lamas, who translate Algebra and Geometry text books into Mongolian, you see, that the seeming contradictions combine in the potentialities of the people, which justly turn toward its glorious past.

To the casual passer-by, Mongolia reveals its outer self, which astonishes one by its wealth of color, its costumes, in which age-old traditions are blended with brilliantly-staged ceremonials. But on closer acquaintance, you will find among the Mongols serious scientific work, a careful investigation of their own country and a desire to send their youth abroad to absorb the methods of contemporary science and technical knowledge. The Mongols go to Germany. They would also like to visit America, but the cost of the journey and of living here, and chiefly, also, their ignorance of the language, are serious obstacles. I must say that during our stay in Mongolia we saw much good in the Mongols. Among many other things, I was pleasantly touched by their serious attitude towards the remains of Mongol antiquity, by their efforts to retain these monuments and by their strictly scientific study of them.

The remarkable discovery by Kozlov's expedition on Mongol territory opened a new page in the history of Siberian antiquity. The same animal designs, which we knew only on metal objects, were discovered on textiles and other material. On the Mongolian territory there are large numbers of kurgans, kereksurs, so-called "deer-stones" and "stone-babas". All these await further study.

In Urga we had to decide the further movements of the expedition. One possibility was to go through China, for, in addition to our passport from the Peking Government, Yang-Tutu had also issued for us a second passport, exactly my height in length! But another circumstance intervened: In Urga we met the representative of the Government of the Dalai-Lama, Lobzang Cholden, who proposed to us that we go through Tibet. Not wishing to intrude, we asked him to confirm his invitation by the written consent of the Lhasa Government. He sent two letters to the Dalai-Lama in Lhasa through Tibetan caravans and also asked the Tibetan representative in Peking to communicate with Lhasa. Three months passed, and Lobzang Cholden, who also was acting consul, informed us that he had received a positive reply via Peking and that he could issue the official passports to us and give us a letter to the Dalai-Lama. As we learned afterwards, these passports are indeed entirely valid. Under the circumstances, we naturally preferred to go through the Gobi and Tibet, instead of risking chance attacks by the Hunhuses in China.

A curious incident should be mentioned. When we were preparing to depart, my son George, drilling our Mongols to use their rifles, took them to the outskirts of the town. As they crept up a slope it appeared that on the other side, a Mongolian infantry detachment was going through the same drill. The sight of both sides meeting each other unexpectedly on the ridge of the hill was most extraordinary. This drill proved to be not at all unnecessary—as our later encounters with the Panagis proved.

On the 13th of April, 1927, our expedition, with the assistance and goodwishes of the Mongolian authorities, set out in a southwestern direction towards the Mongolian frontier post, the Yum-Beise monastery.

A part of the way from Urga, now called Ulan-Bator-Khoto, to Yum-Beise, we covered by motor. The heavily freighted automobiles looked like battle-tanks, and on the top, in yellow, blue and red attire, with coned caps, sat our fellow-travelers, the Buriat and Mongol lamas.

At first we intended to use motors beyond Yum-Beise also. The people told us that we could easily cross the Gobi on them. But this was untrue. The 600 miles more or less, up to Yum-Beise, we covered with difficulty in twelve days, and some days even we did no more than ten to fifteen miles, because of breakages, difficult fordings of rivers and stony ridges. Even here, there was no actual road. Here and there was a camel path, but most of the way was through virgin land, and we had to scout. Two conditions must be remembered. The first, that all existing maps are very indefinite. The second, that one cannot very well trust the local guides. Our guide, an old lama, took us, not to the present-day Yum-Beise, but to an ancient destroyed city, fifty miles to the west. The old man had been confused!

It was evident that we had to abandon our motors

in Yum-Beise. We engaged a caravan from the local monastery which undertook to take us in less than twenty-one days to Shih-pao-ch'eng, between Ansijau and Nanshan. The road from Yum-Beise to Anhsi was interesting, because no traveler before us had used it. It was instructive to investigate how fit it was for travel, in the matters of water supply, fodder and safety. Only the old lama from Yum-Beise knew this road, he assured us, that this direction was far better than the other two, one of which is round about, from the western side, and the other, along the present Chinese road to the east. Recommending this way, he insisted that the one danger of this road—namely the powerful brigand Jalama—had been killed by the Mongols two years ago. And, indeed, in Urga we had seen Jalama's head in alcohol and had heard many tales about this remarkable man.

The Mongolian deserts will guard the legends about Jalama, but no one will ever ascertain what inner motives impelled his strange actions. Jalama was a law graduate from a Russian university, showing unusual abilities. He then went to Mongolia, where he distinguished himself for his activities against the Chinese. He then spent several years in Tibet, studied Lamaism, and also the control of will-power, for which he was naturally equipped. Returning to Mongolia, Jalama received the title, Gun, a title of the Khoshun prince. But he got into difficulties with a Cossack officer and soon found himself in a Russian jail. In the revolution of 1917, he was released. Then followed invasions and activities within Mongolia, after which he gathered round himself a large body of helpers, fortified himself in the Central Gobi and built a city, using as laborers the prisoners of numerous caravans which he had captured. In 1923, a Mongolian officer approached Jalama, as though offering him a friendly gift of a khatik. But under the white silk scarf was a Browning, and the ruler of the desert fell dead, pierced by several bullets. The head of Jalama was carried on a spear around the Mongolian bazaars. After a while his men scattered.

With some excitement, our caravan approached the place where the city of Jalama stood. On the stony slope from far away one can see the white Chorten, made of pieces of quartz—thus Jalama made his prisoners work. The lama advised us to dress in Mongolian kaftans, in order not to attract the attention of any undesirable people we might meet. Tempei-Jaltsen, the city, must be quite near. In the dark night we encamped. In the morning, before sunrise, we heard an unusual commotion. They shouted: "Here, we are right in front of the city!"

We all rushed from our tents and behind the next sandy hill we clearly saw the towers and walls. Neither the Buriats nor the Mongols consented to go and investigate what was in the city. So George and Porten, with carbines, went themselves. The rest awaited, fully ready for battle, watching with field-glasses. Shortly afterwards the two were seen on a tower. This was the sign that the city was deserted. During the day the entire expedition visited the city, in several groups. We all were amazed at Jalama's fantasy in laying out a completely fortified city in the midst of the desert! Certainly he was not a mere brigand! Many songs are being sung about him. And his men have assuredly not disappeared.

The next day some suspicious-looking riders approached our caravan, inquiring about the amount of our arms. But apparently the reply did not encourage them and they dispersed behind the hills.

The region of Mongolia and the Central Gobi awaits explorers and archeologists. Of course, the discoveries of the Andrews Expedition, and the last expedition of Sven Hedin, judging by news accounts, gave excellent results. But the place is so vast, that not one, not two, but only numerous expeditions could completely cover it.

On the way, we encountered many beautiful pieces of so-called "deer-stone", high menhir-like granite or sandstone blocks, sometimes ornamented. We also saw numbers of unexcavated kurgans, large and carefully constructed. The base of the kurgans was symmetrically surrounded by rows of stones, and on the top, also were stones. Near the kurgan, as if forming a second row, were small stone elevations. Especially interesting were the stone "babas", of exactly the same character as those of the southern Russian steppes.

In one case there was a long row of oblong stones, extending almost a whole mile up to a stone "baba", facing the East. We noticed that the carvings even now are smeared with grease and we heard a legend that one of the images was a powerful brigand, who, after his death, was transformed into a protector of this place. Our Tibetan, Konchok, who was attached to us as an attendant by the Tibetan representative in Urga, addressed long prayers to the protector of the region, demanding a happy journey for us. In conclusion, he threw a handful of grain at the image.

* * *

Draw a line from the South Russian steppes and from the northern Caucasus across the steppes of Semipalatinsk, Altai and Mongolia, and then turn South, and you will have the main artery of migration.

The twenty-one days of our travel from Yum-Beise to Shih-pao-ch'eng passed in complete solitude. Besides two or three forsaken yurtas, besides the destroyed Tenpei-Jaltsen and half a dozen suspicious riders, we met only one caravan, which crossed our road on its way from Karakhoto to Hami. The encounter with this caravan almost turned out tragically, for the Chinese head of the caravan, mistaking our camp fires for Jalama's encampment, became alarmed and fired a shot at us from his only rifle.

One thing was quite clear, that the direct way from Yum-Beise to Anhsi-chou is provided with enough water and fodder for the camels and is at present quite safe, although stories of recent robberies are still plentiful. We rejoiced to find in the Gobi numerous most interesting artistic subjects. Firstly, the far-reaching ranges of the Chinese Altai mountains, then the auriferous Altyn-Tagh, give many colorful combinations. One does not see the merciless depression of the Taklamakan, but the multi-colored stone surfaces lend a decisive resonant tone. All springs and wells were in good condition, except one, which was blocked up by the carcass of a khainyck (a kind of yak). On the entire road, beginning with Ladak, the question of water was always most important. The most crystalline streams were filled with carcasses of dead animals, and in the ponds of Sinkiang towns, floated such refuse, that the greatest thirst could not have induced us to drink this concoction.

Outside of Mongolia, we were astonished everywhere by the frequence and monstrous size of goiters, which are caused by the water. We could not ascertain to what extent the boiling of the water helps to obliterate this evil, but certainly this terrible prevalence of goiter must greatly undermine the working capacity of the population.

The clay walls of Anhsi-chou appeared in the distance. A narrow strip of orchards was set near the great Chinese road, which leads from Anhsi-chou to Suchow, and we entered the mountain ranges of Nan-Shan. There already appeared the yurtas of Mongols, who belonged to the Kukunor district. Flocks of cattle were seen. Then the clever Elder of the village, Machen, appeared and under various pretentions extracted quite a lot of money from us. He especially cheated us in exchanging Chinese Dollars to Tibetan Norsangs. We had to buy animals for our new caravan, because the lamas from Yum-Beise were returning home. We also had to buy provisions. Machen assured us that he could only sell for Tibetan

Norsangs, which, he said, were far more valuable than the Chinese Dollars. But it turned out afterwards that things were exactly the opposite and that the value of Norsangs was much lower.

I will not pause to give particulars, of how five of our Buriats, apparently turning insane without reason, went to denounce us to the representative of the Sining Amban, who happened to pass us on the way. The Buriats told him that we were crossing Chinese territory without a Chinese passport and that we went around Anhsi-chou without entering it, for some special purpose. The result of this libel was, that the grey-haired Dungan in his red turban with fifteen soldiers personally came to our camp, and after a long conversation asked to inspect our passports. We satisfied his wish and explained that Anhsi-chou was simply not on our road. The old man became very friendly and offered to beat our accusers with sticks. The slanderers were driven away and their places easily filled by local Mongols.

Of the Mongols of the Kukunor district, whom we met during our stay at Shih-pao-ch'eng, and then at Sharagolji, at the foot of the Humboldt ridge, I can say only good things. When we approached Shih-pao-ch'eng, we met the first Mongol from Kukunor, Rinchino, who raised both hands upwards and greeted us with an unforgettably hearty gesture. Under the same happy sign we lived with the Mongols and parted from them. No difficulties, no quarrel, did they bring to our caravan. True, after our encounter with the Panagis, the old Senge-Lama got frightened and wanted to leave us. But he was so terrified and murmured something in such a friendly way that he soon allowed us to dissuade him.

Mentioning the Mongols, it is necessary to point out some signs of an ancient physical bond between America and Asia. In 1921, when I became acquainted with the Red Indian Pueblos of New Mexico and Arizona, I was forced to exclaim repeatedly: "But those are real Mongols!" Their features, details of their dress, their way of riding, and the character of some of their songs, all carried me away in imagination across the ocean. And now, having the opportunity to study the Mongols of outer and inner Mongolia, I was involuntarily reminded of the Pueblo Indian. Something inexplicable, fundamental, beyond all superficial theories, unites these two nations.

From the Mongols I heard a fairy tale, which emanated from the heart of Mongolia. In a poetic form is related how there lived two brothers on neighboring pieces of land, and how they greatly loved each other. But the fiery Dragon underneath the earth stirred, and the land split and separated both brothers. Their souls yearned for each other. Then they asked the birds to carry their message to their kin. And now they await the heavenly fiery bird to take them across the precipice and to unite the separated ones. In such poetical form is given the tale of cosmic upheaval, which the folk relate in symbols.

With me I had many photographs of the Indians of

New Mexico and Arizona and I showed them in faraway Mongolian encampments. And the Mongols exclaimed: "But those are Mongols!" Thus, the separated brethren recognize each other!

In the lonely yurtas of the Kukunor Mongols one is especially surprised at the paucity of household utensils. Their dress is most effective. Their kaftans remind one, in their picturesque folds, of the Italian frescoes of Gozzoli. The women, with their numerous plaits, with turquoise and silver ornaments, with their red conical hats, look extraordinarily decorative. From their distant encampments, the Mongols came riding on their small horses, to visit our camp. They looked in amazement at our photographs of New York skyscrapers and exclaimed: "The Land of Shambhala!", and they rejoiced at every pin, button or empty fruit tin. Every little household article is a real object of pride for them. And the hearts of these men of the desert are open towards the future!

When the heat of the day grows intense, the guide of the caravan begins to whistle quietly some strange melody. He calls the wind! What a wonderful subject for the theater: "The Seller of Winds"! One also meets the same custom, in the customs of ancient Greece.

In Sharagolji, together with all Mongols of the neighborhood, we experienced the calamity of a flood from the hills. It was the end of July and our camp was near a very small and seemingly most peaceful stream. For three successive nights, from the direction of Ulan Daban on the Humboldt ridge, we continuously heard some unexplainable dull noise. We thought it was the wind. But on the twenty-eighth of July at five p. m., when we were just ready to have our dinner, down the gorge came tremendous torrents, transforming the peaceful little stream into a muddy rumbling force, flooding the whole neighborhood with waves about three feet high. The power of the flood was tremendous. Our kitchen, the dining tent, the tent of our Buriats, were carried away in no time with all their contents. Our boxes were set floating down stream and George's tent was flooded knee-deep. A great variety of our things disappeared on the water, never to be found again. The yurtas of the local Mongols were also destroyed or severely damaged. About two hours later, the river fell and next morning we saw a wet site, entirely transformed. Instead of the barkhans, were deep, water-eaten holes, and instead of level places, were new heaps of sand and stone.

This incident once more confirmed our observations of the alluvial layers of Central Asia. In investigating the profiles of the soil, one is surprised at the comparatively recent origin of many of the upper strata and also at their strange mixture. But such characteristic disturbances as we ourselves have seen, easily change the profiles of the surface. During excavations, such conditions may cause much surprise.

On August 19th, 1927, our caravan preparations were completed. The camels nourished by the grass and bushes, had by then begun to grow new wool. We started across Ulan Daban, deciding to cross dangerous Tsaidam in the shortest direction, thus establishing a new route over Ikhe-Tsaidam and Baga-Tsaidam, to the Neiji Pass. This new route spares the traveler from the western road to Makhai, with its scarcity of water which is so perilous for caravans, and also from the eastern roundabout way, which is very long and which is usually followed by the pilgrims to Lhassa. We were warned that three days of the march would be unpleasant and dangerous, and that for the last twenty-four hours we would have to proceed without a stop, because stopping on the thin surface of the salt deposits is dangerous and also useless, since there is no forage for the animals there. Crossing Tsaidam, we were convinced first, that the complete green outline on the maps does not correspond to reality. The same inaccuracy is also apparent in regard to the names of villages, etc. These places have each a Chinese, Mongolian and Tibetan name, all of which are quite different. Naturally only one of these names gets into the maps, depending on the nationality of the interpreter of previous expeditions. But especially strange are the European names superimposed on ancient places, which have long had their local names. The European names of the mountain ridges of Marco-Polo, Humboldt, Ritter, Alexander III, Prejevalski, have of course no meaning for the local population as they have their own names for these ridges since times immemorable.

Another original circumstance militates against obtaining precise names. The Mongols and Tibetans believe that one should not pronounce the names of places in the desert, otherwise the gods will be attracted by the name and become angry.

We also had to mark in our maps omitted mountain ridges, sandy plains and dry land covered with sharp salt blocks and gaping black openings of swampy water. The green marshes are characteristic only of the lakes of Ikhe and Baga-Tsaidam. Fat horses belonging to the Tsaidam prince graze on these rich meadows. I must mention, that the Tsaidam Prince, who has had some altercations with travelers, showed us complete friendship and even wrote us offering his camels up to Lhassa; but by that time our caravan was already collected.

The crossing of the salt surface of Tsaidam deeply impressed us all. Our guides apparently were fully aware of its dangers, although the season was a favorable one since there are few flies and mosquitoes and very little water in autumn. It felt strange to cross the waterless sandy desert, knowing that to the west began the Kun-Lun upland, which has been so little explored. By and by the sand changed into hard deposits of salt, a heritage of the lake that was here before. The caravan entered into a seemingly endless cemetery of massed sharp salt slabs. The most dangerous part was crossed in darkness, and then, in moonlight. The Mongols shouted: "Don't move from the path!" Indeed, on both sides, among the sharp edges of the salt-slabs could be seen gaping black holes. Even the road was full of holes, and the animals could easily have broken their legs in such holes. The horses walked with great caution. Only one camel fell through the crust. It was pulled out with great difficulty. By morning the salt slabs gradually changed into whitish powdery residue and then the sand began again. Soon the first bushes and tall grass appeared and were greedily seized by our hungry animals. Far in front of us, in blue tones, appeared the mountains. This was Neiji, the geographical border of Tibet, although the frontier outposts were much further.

The march of the blue mountains was through a comparatively fertile region of Teijinor, meaning the land governed by the Council of Elders. The vegetation seemed rich, and the fields were cultivated, but still we noticed deserted encampments, and in the few yurtas we observed commotion. It appeared that a war was on between the Mongols and the Goloks, who lived behind Neiji. We were told that on the road we would see dead bodies. And the people awaited with trepidation, attacks of Tibetan bandits.

There were even vague hints about an attack against our caravan. We recalled the strange incident in Sharagolji: One evening a Mongol came galloping up to our tents at full speed. He was dressed with extraordinary richness. His gold-embroidered costume and his yellow hat with red tassels were most impressive. He quickly entered the nearest tent, which was our doctor's, and, speaking in haste, said that he was our friend, that on the Neiji Pass fifty hostile horsemen were waiting for us. He advised us to go cautiously and to send a patrol ahead. He left as quickly as he had entered, and galloped away, without revealing his name. As we heard the stories about the Panagis and Goloks, we recalled this unexpected, friendly warning.

On the following day, we saw three dead Mongols and the carcass of a horse on the road. On the sandy surface, the traces of a furious race were clearly visible. Taking military precautions, we moved at first along the River Neiji, and then toward the Neiji Pass. In a valley covered by thick brushes three of us noticed the silhouette of a rider and we found a recently built fire and a pipe. We decided not to advance towards the usual pass, a very sandy one affording obstacles, but to change our route and to use the next pass, a few miles further, which bears the same name. This unexpected decision turned out to be a salvation.

The next morning, we started out before sunrise. Mrs. Roerich, who has an extraordinarily sharp ear, heard the distant barking of a dog. But everything remained still. We were about to descend into a narrow gorge between two hills, when peering sharply into the morning mist, we noticed the silhouettes of riders in the gorge. We could distinguish long spears and rifles with gunrests. They were laying for us at the exit of the gorge. But instead of moving on, we retreated to the top of the hill and thus held a commanding position, surprising the enemy. Behind us came our Torguts, the best shooters. From the top of the hill, we saw a group of horsemen, and taking a most advantageous position, we sent our Mongols to warn them, that should they continue hostilities, we would spare neither their lives nor their yurtas. The negotiations were successful.

The Panagis again spoke of having sent for fifty men, and a few hours later we saw their herds coming back from the mountains to their yurtas, which meant that measures had been taken just in time. The next day, in full battle formation and followed by suspicious looking horsemen, we crossed the Neiji Pass. Here a terrible thunderstorm and heavy snowfall broke out, quite unusual for the month of September. The Mongols said: "The Mountain-god Lo is angry because the Panagis intended to harm great people. In the snow they will never attack us, because traces would remain on the ground."

In front of us was the Marco-Polo ridge, the stern Angar-Dakchin, and beyond, the picturesque Kokushili and the mighty Dungbure. One might write an entire volume of these places alone; of the huge herds of wild yaks numbering many hundreds; of white-collared bears which come up most trustingly; of wolves attacking wild goats and antelopes. One may notice mineral springs, hot geysers and other surprises of this unusual nature which amaze one.

From Tsaidam, which is eight to nine thousand feet high, we ascended the Tibetan upland to about fourteen to fifteen thousand feet.

Here occurred characteristic episodes in our negotiations with the Tibetans, which I will now describe:

On the twentieth of September our caravan noticed with some excitement the tent of the first Tibetan post. Several ragged people, in dirty sheep-skin kaftans, approached us and demanded our passport. In the presence of ample witnesses we handed them our Tibetan passport, and they allowed us to proceed. The passport was sent to their chief.

On October sixth, the Tibetans proposed that we stop in a small place named Shindi, to await further sanction from the Tibetan General Khapshopa, the high commissioner of Hors and the Commander of the northern Tibetan frontier. Two days later our camp was moved closer to the general's headquarters, on the river Chunargen.

This place will forever remain in our memory. The dull upland, arctic in character, was full of small mounds and was bordered by the drear outlines of sliding hills. The general's first welcome was the acme of kindness and friendliness. He told us that in consideration of our passports and letter, he would permit us to proceed to Lhasa via Nagchu. Nagchu is the northern fort of Tibet and is three days from Chunargen. The general asked us only to stop for three days and to move our camp nearer to his headquarters, as he wanted personally to inspect our things. "The hands of small people", he explained, "should not touch the belongings of great people!"

He then said, that he would remain with us until the sanction to proceed arrived and in my honor he ordered a special solemn retreat to be played by his band every evening. Apparently the general had more musicians with drums, clarinets and Scotch bagpipes, than soldiers. When we visited him, they gave us a cannon salute and paraded all their banners. The strange soldiers, in dirty jackets with torn buttons, held their rifles in every-which direction. In all, our meetings with the general were very friendly, and probably he was not guilty of what followed. When a week passed, still without reply, the general informed us that he had to depart on duty, but that he was leaving a major and five soldiers with us and would give all necessary instructions to the local elders of the Hors.

The general left, and instead of three days we remained in this dull place, at 15,000 altitude, for five months. The situation became catastrophic. A severe winter set in, with whirlwinds and snow. What had happened, and where, we could not discover, for all letters sent by us to the Dalai-Lama and Governor of Nagchu, were returned to us and often torn up. We repeatedly wrote to the American Consul in Calcutta, to the British Resident, Colonel Bailey in Gangtok and to our Institutions in New York, requesting the Governor of Nagchu to send all this by wire from Lhasa to India. And we were told that the telegraph between Lhasa and India no longer existed—a downright lie!

Through the major, we asked permission either to return back or to proceed to the general's headquarters, but they refused us permission either to go forward or back, as if they actually wished our destruction. Our money was exhausted. Of course the American dollars which we had with us, were absolutely useless. Moreover, we had no more medicine and our provisions were at an end. Under our very eyes, the whole caravan perished. Each night the freezing, starved animals approached our tents, as though knocking for the last time before their death. And in the morning we found them dead, near our tents. Our Mongols dragged them beyond the camp, where packs of wild dogs and condors and vultures were already awaiting their prey. Of a hundred-and-two animals, we lost ninety-two. On the Tibetan uplands, we also left the bodies of five of our fellow-travelers: three lamas, one a Buriat and two Mongols, then Champa, the Tibetan, and finally the Tibetan major's wife who died of inflammation of the lungs. Even the natives could not withstand the severe conditions. Our caravan had only summer tents, as we never imagined we would pass the winter in Changthang, which is considered the most severe site in Asia.

Mrs. Roerich's pulse reached 145, and our doctor called it "the pulse of a bird". My pulse was 130, instead of the usual 64. The pulses of George and the two Bogdanovs remained about 120. The doctor prophesied the most dark prospects and wrote medical certificates, stating that to detain an expedition under such conditions, was equal to an attempt at murder.

Of this stay in Nagchu I could write a whole book, full of the saddest reminiscences.

There were two governors of Nagchu, one was considered a trusted aide of the Dalai-Lama and was himself a lama, although he had a family. To describe them, it is sufficient to relate two short episodes which they themselves told us:

One episode concerns General Laden-La, a general of the Tibetan army, an undoubtedly gifted personality, to whom at one time was entrusted the reform of the mixed troops of Tibet. The lama-governor informed us that Laden-La had been dismissed from the army because he introduced "red" customs by recommending European uniforms for the soldiers and ordering the salutation of men to officers.

The same governor explained the Russian revolution thus: "There lived a man named Nenin, who did not like the white Tzar. Nenin took a pistol and shot the Tzar, and then climbed a high tree and proclaimed that the customs would be red and that the churches would be closed. But there was a woman, the sister of the Tzar, who knew both red and white customs. She took a pistol and shot Nenin!"

It would be too long to relate all our negotiations with the drunken major, and later with the governors of Nagchu. In any case, on March sixth, we finally started for India, compelled to go by the most difficult, circuitous way. With us, went also the unsolved problems as to how the Government of Lhasa could refuse to recognize the passport issued by its own official and whether one could detain a peaceful American expedition, with three women members an entire winter in summer tents at the most disastrous heights, and why it was necessary for the Tibetans to imperil our health, starve the entire caravan to death and destroy all our cinema films through acute changes of temperature.

Changthang—the northern upland of Tibet—truly deserves its fame as the coldest spot in Asia. Terrific storms increase to a tremendous degree the effect of the frost, and the rare atmosphere at fifteen to sixteen thousand feet, makes the conditions exceptionally severe. One may imagine the temperature, when our brandy froze in a closed bottle! What temperature is required to freeze strong alcohol? Of course, by eleven o'clock in the morning the sun warms the atmosphere considerably, but after sunset and by night, and especially in the early hours before sunrise, the frost is unbearable. Our doctor had the unusual opportunity to investigate from a medical point of view the conditions on these exceptional uplands.

After Nagchu-Dzong our way passed Tengri-Nor to Shentsa-Dzong, and then across several passes to Saga-Dzong. From there we went along the Brahmaputra river to the border of Nepal to Tingri-Dzong. Shekar-Dzong and Kampa Dzong were the last points of our two-and-a-half months' trip to the Himalayan pass, Sepo La. Passing Sepo La, we descended by way of Thangu to Gangtok, the capital of Sikkim, where we were greeted most heartily by the British Resident, Lt.-Colonel Bailey, his wife and the Maharajah of Sikkim. On the 26th of May, 1928, we arrived in Darjeeling, staying again in the villa Talai-Pho-Brang, to compile the artistic and scientific material we had gathered.

* * *

Now let us cast a brief glance at the characteristics of contemporary life in Tibet and at its art:

Tibet offers the most astonishing combination of contradictions.

On one side, we saw profound knowledge and remarkably developed psychic energy. On the other, complete ignorance and limitless darkness.

On one side, there is devotion to religion, even in its limited form. On the other side, we noticed how the money donated to monasteries was concealed and how false oaths were given in the name of the "three Pearls of the Teaching".

On one side, we saw respect toward women and their exemption from hard work. On the other side, there exists the institution of polyandry, so absurd in our times; it is strange to think that polyandry can exist side by side with Buddhism, even with its lamaistic form.

On one side, we saw, instead of palaces, poor clay huts. But, on the other hand, the Tibetan governors call these huts beautiful snowy palaces, unashamed of such hyperboles.

On one side, the government of Lhasa calls itself the "Government victorious in all directions". But on the other side, we see this inscription on the miserable copper coins—the sho. We saw neither gold nor silver, either in the dzongs, or in the hands of the people. It is also curious that the half and quarter sho, which are also copper, are larger than the sho itself. The entire population prefers silver rupees or silver Mexican dollars, to their own Tibetan sho. The people even quote two prices when selling goods: a higher price if payment is made in Tibetan shos and a considerably lower one if paid in rupees and Chinese silver. But with

Chinese silver it is not always easy either. In some places they demand Imperial coins; in other places, the Republican coins with six letters, or with seven. So that a whole assortment of various currencies is required.

But we were not surprised, as we were already accustomed to strange currency since our visit to Sinkiang, where the wooden signs issued by the gambling houses in some places are valued more highly than the local paper money. In Sinkiang, the greater part of the notes often consists of advertisements of soap and other products glued underneath. We even received such notes from the governmental Treasury, which the neighboring Amban acknowledged were not valid.

The entire life of Tibet seems composed of contradictions.

After the picturesque cities and monasteries of Ladak, we looked in vain for something more beautiful in Greater Tibet. We passed ancient dzongs, monasteries and villages. If from afar, the silhouettes at times looked good, on approach we were grieved to see the poverty and shoddiness of Tibetan structures. It is true that on the mountains and along the river bed of the Brahmaputra are towers dating from the time of the ancient Tibetan kings. In these structures one feels the power of creative thought. And one frequently sees these ruins. Near them are usually the remains of once-cultivated fields. But that is all of the past. It all speaks of a life now gone, now passed.

Saga-Dzong is a poor village with brittle clay walls.

Black tents, like spiders, are pitched on long black ropes. And like a spider's web over the village, hangs a mass of torn and dirty flags. There is as much dirt as in Nagchu-Dzong. I remember how in Nagchu, when we pointed out the dreadful dirt of the city, the donier of the governor replied: "If you consider this dirty, what would you say of Lhasa?" Tingri-Dzong, though considered the largest fortress on the Nepalese frontier, amazed us by its wretchedness and uselessness for defense. Tinkiu, Shekar and Kampa-Dzong are impressive only in those parts, where something is left from ancient times. But the things of antiquity decay and are replaced by clay walls. Dzong-pens, the commanders of the castles, no longer live on the summits, but seek shelter lower on the hill.

Regarding the local life, our compulsory five months' stay in the land of the Hors, and the long journey in Northern, Western, Central and Southern Tibet, provided us with a mass of material. For the first time an expedition had no need of an interpreter, as even the Tibetans themselves affirm that George knows Tibetan better than Sir Charles Bell, who is considered an authority on the language. Without personal knowledge of the language, it is of course rash to judge the conditions of the country. The journey from Chunargen to the Sikkim frontier might fill an entire volume.

We went on so-called Urton (locally hired) yaks. Before our minds we reviewed the entire vista of contradictions between the people and the officials of Lhasa. And the impression strengthened, that a part of the lamas and the people are on one side and the group of Lhasa officials are on the other. Of the latter, even the Tibetans themselves said, that "their hearts are blacker than coal and harder than stone."

We set up our camp not far from the camps of the Golokis. Both camps distrusted each other. The entire night one could hear the call: "Ki-hoho!" from the side of the Golokis. And our Hors reply "Khoi-khe!" Thus, through the entire night, they warned each other of the sleepless vigilance of the camp.

In Tingri-Dzong, which is considered the second largest fort after Shigatse, our chief-of-transport discovered on one of our yaks a strange object, wrapped in red silk. We investigated his discovery and it turned out, that with our caravan had been sent an arrow, on which was wrapped an order for mobilization of the local troops, to suppress a riot in Poyul, in Eastern Tibet. Instead of sending the urgent order by special courier, the people attach the order to the yak of a private caravan, which may perhaps do but ten miles a day.

Near Saga-Dzong the elders refused to recognize the passport of the Dalai-Lama, sent to us from Lhasa. They stated that they had nothing in common with the Government of Lhasa. One can remember endless similar circumstances taken from life, and recounted around the caravan camp fires, when the Tibetans ate their raw meat.

The Dalai-Lama is regarded as an incarnation of Avolokiteshvara and a guardian of the true Teaching of Buddha. At the same time, throughout Tibet is related a prophecy which emanates from the Tenjye-ling monastery, stating that the present and thirteenth Dalai-Lama is the last one.

Concerning the omniscience of the Dalai-Lama, many funny stories are told by the people and lamas. For instance, a high lama, who had free access to the Dalai-Lama, once visited the Dalai-Lama, and had just put his foot through the door, when the Dalai-Lama asked, "Who is there?" Then the lama stretched his hand inside the door. Again the Dalai-Lama asked, "Who is there?" Thereupon, the lama entered with a bow, saying: "Your Holiness uselessly troubles to put this question. In accordance with your omniscience you should know who was behind the door".

During our negotiations with the governors of Nagchu, in answer to their queries, we told them several times, "But you have a State oracle in Lhasa, why not ask it about us?" Whereupon both governors looked at each other and laughed.

An entirely different attitude may be noticed everywhere toward the Tashi-Lama, whose name is always pronounced with deep reverence.

"The customs of Panchen Rinpoche are entirely different", the Tibetans used to say.

The Tibetans await the fulfilment of the prophecy about the return of the Tashi-Lama, when he will reconstruct Tibet and the precious teaching will again flourish.

Of the flight of the Tashi-Lama from Tibet in 1923, people speak everywhere with special significance and reverence. They tell of remarkable incidents which accompanied this heroic exodus. It is told that when the Tashi-Lama was being pursued near the northwestern lakes, the armed detachment from Lhasa almost overtook and captured him. A long road around the lake faced the Tashi-Lama, and his men became excited. But the spiritual Leader of Tibet remained undisturbed and gave instructions that the caravan should stop over night before the lake. During the night a severe frost set in and the lake was covered by thick ice, over which they crossed, thus shortening their way considerably. In the meantime the sun rose, the ice melted, and when the pursuers reached the lake, it was impossible to cross and the Lhasa detachment was detained for several days.

Following the road indicated to us, we went for some time along the same way, by which the Tashi-Lama had fled, and it was significant to hear the rumors of the people and the general anticipation of the return of the spiritual Ruler of Tibet. For it is the Tashi-Lama, whose name is connected with the conception of Shambhala.

The Tibetans themselves tell you all this and point out that the Lhasa officials afford prosperity neither to the people nor the religion.

Let us glance at several pictures from life, in order to understand how the contemporary state of religion in Tibet needs purification.

Here high lamas make their pecuniary calculations on their sacred rosaries. Is this permitted? They turn their prayer wheels by water and windmills and even clock works, releasing themselves from expending any energy. Does this represent the commandment of Buddha?

Not far from the government dzong stands the object of the latest idol worship—a high stone smeared with fat. It appears that the Lhasa government itself has sanctioned this place of prayer in honor of the government oracle!

It is prohibited to kill animals. This is splendid. But the storerooms of the monasteries are filled with carcasses of mutton and yak. We were told of the sinless method of killing cattle,—driving the animals to the edge of steep cliffs, where they fall down and kill themselves.

In the corner of a shop sits a lama, the owner, and turns his prayer wheel. On the wall are images of Shambhala and Tsong-Kha-pa. And right next to them, are huge earthen pots full of the local wine, which the lama makes to intoxicate his people.

Some one connected with a high personage offers us a talisman for sale, with "complete guarantee" of its invulnerability against fire-arms. He offers it to us for three hundred rupees. In view of the complete guarantee he offers, we suggest that the fortunate owner should try it out on himself. But the believer from Lhasa proposes to convince us with the aid of a goat, continuing to assure us of the miraculous powers of the talisman. When we do not agree to let him try it on the poor goat, the Tibetan walks off indignantly.

To deprive the criminal of further incarnations is considered the severest form of punishment. To effect this, the heads of the worst criminals are cut off and dried in a special place where an entire collection of similar remains is preserved.

Near the sacred mendangs and temples are scattered dead dogs, and sacred inscriptions are covered with human excrement. On the road and on the fields, are thrown the sacred inscriptions. Many stupas have crumpled to pieces and many temples have been forsaken.

Not far from Lhasa is a place where corpses are hacked apart and thrown to vultures, dogs and pigs to be devoured. It is customary to roll naked on these remains to preserve one's good health. The Buriat Tsibikoff, in his book on Tibet, assures his readers that His Holiness the Dalai-Lama has himself performed this absurd ritual.

Most remarkable is the testimony of the Tibetans about "Rolang"—the resurrection of the dead. Everywhere one hears of "revived corpses, which jump up and, possessed of extraordinary strength, kill people."

The Tibetans claim that whoever poisons a person of high estate, himself receives the wealth and happiness of the poisoned person. There exist families, in which the right to poison is handed down as a privilege of birth. These families preserve the secret of a special poison. For this reason, friendly Tibetans always advise one to be extremely cautious with other people's food. One can hear of cases, where people were poisoned with tea and food that was sent to their homes as a sign of special esteem. This reminds one of old tales of poisoned objects and especially rings. We saw daggers and rings with special devices for carrying poison.

Of such pictures from the real life of Tibet, one can mention many. They all reveal how many aspects of the religion must be cleansed and reformed. But we know many highly distinguished lamas and we hope that they can effect an enlightened reform of Tibet.

"Why do our people lie so much?" worries a Tibetan on the banks of the Brahmaputra. This vice must also be erased.

It is said that the Tashi-Lama is at present in Mongolia, corroborating a Mandala of the Buddhist Teaching. From this one should expect good results, as Tibet is much in need of spiritual purification.

In speaking of religions in Tibet, one should mention also the Black Faith, inimical to Buddha. As we were able to convince ourselves, in addition to the Gelukpa, to the Red-Cap Sect of Padma Sambhava, and many other branches, the Bon-po or Black Faith, is also spread considerably in Tibet. And it is much more widely spread than one would imagine. We have even heard that Bon-po is on the increase. We saw a great many monasteries of the Bon-po in different parts of Tibet. They all are apparently very wealthy. In Sharugen we were received most cordially in the Bon-po monastery, and were even admitted into the temple and shown the sacred books. It was proposed to George that he read them. But then suddenly their attitude changed. It appeared that the Bon-po had heard of our interest in Buddhism and therefore regarded us as their enemies.

The Bon-po say that the Buddhists are their enemies. Buddha is not recognized and the Dalai-Lama is considered only a temporal ruler. The ceremonials are conducted in a way precisely contrary to those of the Buddhists. The sign of the Svastika is represented in an inverted direction. The processions in the temple walk away from the sun. Instead of Buddha, another protector is represented, whose biography coincides strangely with the narratives of Buddha's life. The Bon-po have their own sacred books. It is a pity that the literature of the Black Faith has been studied so little and that their sacred books have not yet been translated. One cannot refer to these ancient traditions lightly, when they speak of their mysterious "Gods of Svastika." The ancient solar and fire cults undoubtedly are the basis of Bon-po, and one must carefully examine these old, half-erased signs.

Both with regard to Bon-po and with regard to its archæological remains, Tibet has not yet been sufficiently explored. We especially rejoiced in discovering in the Trans-Himalayan region of Tibet, typical menhirs and cromlechs. You can picture yourself how remarkable it is to see the long rows of stones, or stone circles, which vividly transport you to Carnack and the coast of Bretagne. After their long journey, the prehistoric druids recalled their distant homes. The ancient Bon-po in some way may be connected with these menhirs. In any case, this discovery rounded out our search for traces of the great migrations.

Details of the costumes and arms of the Tibetans also give rise to significant comparisons. Let us take the ancient swords of the Tibetans and see whether there is no resemblance to some of the swords from Gothic burial grounds. Let us take fibulæ, shoulder buckles, and compare them with those of the Alan and Gothic burial places in South Russia and Europe. Before me is a fibula with a double-headed eagle exactly of the same stylization as was found on the Kuban. Here is another Tibetan buckle from Derge of ancient workmanship, with a lion at the foot of a mountain and with stylized flowers around. Take the Scythian buckle found by Kozlov, which is of the same size, and you will be surprised to see the same concepts. Besides menhirs and cromlechs in the region of Shenza-Dzong, we also found ancient burial places in the Trans-Himalayas, which recalled the Altai burial places and the graves of the Southern steppes. It is a pity that excavations are not possible in Tibet, as the people pretend that Buddha prohibited touching the depths of the earth.

In the same district of the Trans-Himalayas, called Doring—Long Stone, apparently because of the ancient menhirs—we saw a woman's head-gear, quite unusual for Tibet. It was exactly the Slavonic kokoshnik, red as usual, adorned with turquoise and silver coins or ornamented with beads. Neither to the north or south of here did we again see such head-gear. Apparently some special tribal remnants have survived here. Their language does not differ from the other northern mixed dialects. In general the Tibetan dialects are a problem, for besides the basic Lhasa dialect, every region retains its own dialect, and these are so different that the Tibetans of Lhasa at times cannot understand their own people.

There were two other interesting analogies. When I showed a Tibetan a unicorn from a coat of arms, he was not surprised, but insisted that in Tibet there was and still exists near the region of K'am an antelope with one horn. Some Tibetans even volunteered to procure such an antelope for us, should we stop in Tibet. The unicorn is also found on Chinese and Tibetan tankas. The British explorer Bryan Hodson has exported a specimen of a special antelope with one horn. Thus, the heraldic myth becomes reality near the Himalayas.

Another interesting object, which we saw in different parts of Tibet, is the sacred bead, the dzi or zi. One distinguishes two types of these beads. One is a Chinese imitation, the other is the ancient bead, valued very highly in Tibet, sometimes as high as 1500 rupees each. Miraculous power is attributed to the dzi. We were told, that during the tilling of the fields, the beads jump out of the ground. People say that the dzi is a hardened dart of lightning or the excrement of a heavenly bird. The value of the dzi varies according to the number of signs on it. The bead looks like a piece of horn, with some special signs on it. It is interesting that a similar bead was found during the excavations in Taxila, among antiques of a period not later than the first century of our era. Thus, the age of the dzi is correctly estimated by the Tibetans. Perhaps they were ancient talismans or terraphim.

It should also not be forgotten that the Catholic missionary, Odorico de Pardenone, who visited Tibet in the fourteenth century, stated that Lhasa or even the entire country, was called Gota. Let us remember the legendary kingdom of the Gotls.

In order to conclude our analogies, let us recall, without drawing any conclusions, that the tribes of Northern Tibet, called the Hors, remind one strongly of some European types. There is nothing Chinese, Mongolian or Hindu in them. Before you, somewhat modified, pass faces as though from portraits of old French, Dutch and Spanish artists.

Inhabitants of Lyons, Basques, Italians, seem to look at you, with large straight eyes, aquiline noses and characteristic wrinkles, thin lips and long black locks of hair. This question promises to provide most interesting comparisons.

Let us now glance at the art of Tibet. This art begins to be truly appreciated with full justification. Even further, let us predict that the appreciation of ancient Tibetan art will increase still more.

The paintings, tankas or frescoes, of an earlier period than the nineteenth century, afford one the greatest delight. We do not insist that there is any special Tibetan style. Of course, in the art of Tibet we always recognize a blending with old China, India or Nepal, as the first image of Buddha came to Tibet in the sixth century from China and Nepal. But the Chinese and Hindu sources were so exquisite, that the blending of them results in a highly artistic composite.

But in the nineteenth century, the art became mechanical. There began the stenciled weak repetition of the fine old forms. Therefore, in judging Tibetan art, let us consider that at present, during the transition, there is no proper art and creativeness in Tibet. The Tibetans themselves understand very well, that their old workmanship is superior to the present, in every respect. But even in this conclusion, there is no inevitable judgment.

The experienced eye may observe, that new values are entering life, though reticently. Let us hope that the present transition of Tibet will resolve in a rational approach to true values.

The enlightened lamas will find means to raise the religion once again to the true commandments of Buddha. The people will find application for their abilities, for the Tibetan people are naturally very able. The creative power of Tibet will eschew all stencilized repetitions and the lotus of knowledge and beauty will blossom and illumine the country.

Architecture in Tibet also suggests many unusual possibilities, such for instance as the old Tibetan strongholds, beginning with the chief and principal building of Tibet—the seventeen-story Potala. Are similar structures not adaptable to improvement and do they not approach our skyscrapers?

At present in Lhasa electric light has been prohibited on the streets, moving pictures are prohibited, sewing machines are prohibited, European footwear is prohibited. Again Tibet has prohibited its laymen from cutting their hair. If the higher military officials cut their hair, they are demoted. The people have again been ordered to wear long khalats, most inconvenient for work, as well as Tibetan-Chinese footwear.

The "Statesman" of February 17th, 1929, states in connection with the proposed fourth Mount Everest expedition: "If it was difficult to obtain permission from Tibet previously, then at present this is entirely impossible. Further, the inhabitants of the Arun valley, who have made good money on foreigners, are against the latter entering the valley for a fourth time. People say, that when the expedition of 1924 returned to India, the Dalai-Lama fell ill for a day. Careful investigations were made all over Tibet to find out where the lama-monks had broken their vow, and it was found that a monk of the Arun valley had eaten fish. As a justification of this deed, which had endangered the life of the Dalai-Lama, the monk could but say that he became terribly excited on seeing foreigners near the monastery."

I remember a story about three hens. In our caravan we had three hens, which, despite their daily travels in a basket on a camel's back, continued to lay regularly. After our detention in Nagchu, we had nothing to feed them and we gave them to the Tibetan major. The disappearance of the hens from our camp was at once reported to the governor of Nagchu and an entire correspondence ensued about the hens eaten by foreigners. The major had to sign a written statement that the hens were still alive. It is strange that one may not eat fish and birds, nor kill a mad dog nor a dangerous condor, but that one may kill a yak or a sheep, not only for the use of laymen, but even for lamas.

We think that it was not the fish eaten by the lama which caused the illness of the Dalai-Lama, but more probably the unspeakable dirt, with which some monasteries are "ornamented". Why must lamas have black shiny faces and arms? We were shocked to see these coal-black people, with so open an aversion to water. I can well imagine how difficult it must be for the Tashi-Lama and the enlightened lamas to influence the black, self-satisfied masses. For it is pure ignorance which provokes self-satisfaction and self-content.

All these evidences of dirt, untruth and hypocrisy were not bequeathed by the Blessed Buddha! The Teaching of Buddha foresees first of all self-improvement and progress. But the prohibitions of which I speak above indicate, first of all, a blunt adoration of the old. But in such retrogression one may easily reach the incoherence of our forefathers. The past is good so long as it does not impede the future. But what would happen if the death of the beautiful past has been allowed, and the future prohibited?

Tibet has presumed for itself spiritual supremacy over its neighbors. The Tibetans look aloofly on Sikkimese, Ladakis, Kalmucks and call the Mongols their own bondsmen. Yet all these people are growing in consciousness. But Tibet tries forcibly to arrest the steps of evolution. And yet one notes how the Tibetan people themselves are attracted to everything enhancing comfort and which lightens work.

I make these observations with no desire to belittle the Tibetans. I have often had occasion to note the keenness, flexibility and working ability of these people. We had several Tibetans in our house and were quite satisfied with them and parted as friends. Mrs. Roerich had a Tibetan aya, who was most useful and with much dignity coöperated in our household. Knowing these fine sides of the Tibetan nature, one can only regret that people do not receive sufficient guidance, and that those who could guide them are not permitted to do so. The heart of Tibet is beating and the temporary paralysis of some of its organs will pass. For in the ancient history of Tibet we find glorious though short pages. Let us remember that Tibetan conquerors reached Kashgar and went beyond Kukunor. Let us remember that the fifth Dalai-Lama bestowed flourishing prosperity on his country and crowned it with the Potala, which up to now remains the only significant building of Tibet. Let us not forget that a whole succession of Tashi-Lamas left behind them monuments of enlightenment and that it is the Tashi-Lamas who are united with the conception of Shambhala.

The temporary obscurity will disappear, and those who once knew how to build eagles' nests on the summits, will again remember the glorious days of bygone Tibet and will find a solution for them in the present.

* * *

The last pass is Sepo La. It is the easiest of all. We pass a turquoise blue lake—the source of the Lachen river. In a diminutive stream the torrent begins and after a journey of two days it begins to roar and is so grown that one can no longer cross without a bridge. We sense the fragrance of the healing Balu and the first stubby cedars. Once again we see rhododendron before us. We are in Sikkim.

Again, files of bronze, half-naked Sikkimese, with garlands on their heads, carry baskets full of tangerines on their backs. The noisy monkeys whistle in the trees. Blue butterflies, large as birds, fly ahead of us. Everything is a rich varied green. From above, crowned by rainbow clouds, fall cascades.

Near the Tishta river, two leopards appear on the road. They look at us peacefully and with their soft step disappear again in the jungle.

The Himalayas intercept the view of Tibet. Where else is there such brilliance, such spiritual plenty, if not among these precious snows! Nowhere else does there exist such descriptive language as in Sikkim; to every word is added the conception of heroes: men-heroes, women-heroes, hero-rocks, hero-trees, hero-waterfalls, hero-eagles.

Not only are spiritual summits concentrated in the Himalayas, but physical wealth as well gives to this snow-land its great fame. Throughout the world, is known the legend of the Fire-blossom. In China, Mongolia, Siberia, Serbia, Norway, Bretagne, one may hear of the miraculous fire-blossom. And where does the source of this legend lead one? To the Himalayas themselves!

On the Himalayas grows a special species of black aconite. The natives say they gather it by night when it glows and can thus be distinguished from other species of aconite. Verily, the Fire-blossom grows on the Himalayas!

The Hindu sings: "Can I speak of the grandeur of the Creator, when I know the incomparable Beauty of the Himalayas!"

Part II

SHAMBHALA

II

SHAMBHALA

You may ask me what conception was the most uplifting for me among the innumerable impressions. Without hesitation I reply: "Shambhala!"

If I pronounce for you the most sacred word of Asia, Shambhala, you will be silent. If I pronounce the same name in Sanskrit, Kalapa, you will be silent. Even if I tell you the name of the mighty Ruler of Shambhala, Rigden Jyepo, this thundering name of Asia will not move you. But you are not at fault. All the indications about Shambhala are scattered in literature and not one book has as yet been written in any of the Western languages about this stronghold of Asia. But if you wish to be understood in Asia and to approach her as a welcome guest, you must meet your host with the most sacred word. You must show that these conceptions are not mere empty sounds for you but that you value them and can coördinate them with the highest concepts of evolution.

Baradiin, the Buriat scholar, in his latest book on the monasteries of Mongolia and Tibet, states, among other things, that recently in China and Mongolia, monasteries in honor of Shambhala were founded and that in some of the existing monasteries special *datsans* of Shambhala have been instituted.

To the casual onlooker this information may no doubt sound metaphysical and abstract, or unimportant. To the superficial observer such news, drowned in the day's political and commercial speculations, may seem but another seed of superstition, devoid of reality.

But the attentive observer, who has traversed the depths of Asia, will feel quite otherwise. For him, this news will be full of importance, full of significance for the future. In this brief information, the person familiar with all the sources and waves of Asia, will feel again how vital to Asia are all the so-called prophecies and legends, emanating from the most ancient origins. The oldest Vedas, the younger Puranas and an entire literature, of most varied sources, affirm the extraordinary meaning of the mysterious word, Shambhala for Asia.

Both in the large populous centers, where sacred conceptions are pronounced with a cautious glance, and in the limitless deserts of the Mongolian Gobi, the word Shambhala, or the mysterious Kalapa of the Hindus, sounds like the most realistic symbol of the great Future. In these words about Shambhala, in the narratives, legends, songs and folklore, is contained what is perhaps the most important message of the East. He who as yet knows nothing of Shambhala, cannot state that he has studied the East and knows contemporary Asia.

Before speaking of Shambhala proper, let us remember the Messianic conceptions which are to be found among the most varied peoples of Asia and which unite them into one great future expectation.

The yearning of Palestine towards a Messiah is well known. The anticipation of a great Avatar near the Bridge of the Worlds exists throughout broad masses. People know of the White Horse and the Fiery Comet-like Sword and the radiant advent of the Great Rider above the skies. The learned rabbis and Kabalists throughout Palestine, Syria, Persia and the whole of Iran, relate remarkable things on this subject.

The Moslems of Persia, Arabia, Chinese Turkestan, sacredly preserve the legend of Muntazar, who will soon lay the foundation of a New Era. It is true that when you speak to the Mullahs of Muntazar, they will sharply deny it at first, but if you insist sufficiently and show sufficient knowledge, they will gradually cease their denials and often even add many important details. And if you still persist and tell them that they have already saddled the white horse in Isphahan, which is to carry the Great Comer, the Mullahs will look at each other and add that in Mecca a Great Tomb is already prepared for the Prophet of the Truth.

The most learned Japanese, the great scholars, speak highly of the awaited Avatar, and the learned Brahmins, taking their information from the Vishnu Puranas and the Devi Puranas, quote beautiful lines about the Kalki Avatar coming on a white horse.

For the moment I shall not touch any of the inner signs which have gathered round the conception of Shambhala.

To transmit a more realistic impression I first want to relate how and where we came in contact with people who know and are devoted to the Great Conception of Asia. We knew already about Shambhala. We had already read the translation by Professor Grunwedel of the Tibetan manuscript, "Road to Shambhala," written by the Third Tashi-Lama, one of the most esteemed high priests of Tibet.

First, then, let us examine the milestones which greeted us during our travels:

In the Temple of Ghum monastery, not far from the Nepalese frontier, instead of the usual central figure of Buddha, you see a huge image of the Buddha-Maitreya, the coming Saviour and Ruler of Humanity. This image is like the great image of Maitreya in Tashi-Lhunpo near Shigatse, seat of the spiritual ruler of Tibet, the Tashi-Lama. The Lord Maitreya is seated on his throne; his legs are no longer crossed as usual, but are already set on the ground. This is a sign that the time of His Coming is near and that the Ruler is already preparing to descend from his throne. This monastery was built about twenty years ago by a learned Mongolian lama, who came from distant Mongolia to Tibet. Crossing the Himalayas and Sikkim, where the red sect of Padma Sambhava is the official religion, he came to erect this new monastery and to proclaim the approaching advent of the Lord Maitreya.

In 1924, a learned lama, the faithful disciple of the founder of the monastery, who had shared with him the profound Teaching and many prophecies for the future, told us before the impressive image: "Verily, the time of the great advent is nearing. According to our prophecies, the epoch of Shambhala has already begun. Rigden Jyepo, the Ruler of Shambhala, is already preparing his unconquerable army for the last fight. All his assistants and officers are already incarnating.

"Have you seen the tanka-banner of the Ruler of Shambhala and his fight against all evil forces? When our Tashi-Lama fled from Tibet recently, he took with him only a few banners, but among them were several banners about Shambhala. Many learned lamas fled from Tashi-Lhunpo and recently there arrived from Tibet a geshe (learned) painter, a gelong of Tashi-Lhunpo. He knows how to paint the tanka of Shambhala. There are several variations of this subject, but you should have the one with the battle in the foreground."

Shortly after, the lama-artist, Lariva, was seated on a rug in the white gallery of our home, outlining the complicated composition on the white surface of the specially prepared canvas. In the middle was the Mighty Ruler of Shambhala in the glory of His majestic abode. Below, wages a terrific battle, in which the enemies of the righteous Ruler are unmercifully destroyed. In dedication, the banner is adorned by the following inscription: "To the Illustrious Rigden, King of Northern Shambhala."

It was touching to observe with what respect and veneration the lama-artist worked. When he pronounced the name of the Ruler of Shambhala, he clasped his hands as if in prayer.

At the time of our arrival in Sikkim, the Tashi-Lama had fled from Tashi-Lhunpo to China. Everyone was startled by this unprecedented movement of the spiritual head of Tibet. The Lhasa government, in confusion, began searching everywhere, but rumors were already circulating that the Tashi-Lama had passed through Calcutta in disguise.

Referring to this event a lama said to us: "Verily, the old prophecies are fulfilled. The time of Shambhala has come. For centuries and centuries, it has been predicted that before the time of Shambhala, many wonderful events would occur, many terrible wars would take place and Panchen Rinpoche would leave his abode in Tashi-Lhunpo in Tibet. Verily, the time of Shambhala has come. The great war has devastated countries, many thrones have perished, earthquakes have destroyed the old temples of Japan and now our revered Ruler has left his country."

Following their spiritual ruler, one of the most esteemed high priests, Geshe Rinpoche from Chumbi, whom the Tibetans regard as an incarnation of Tsong-Kha-Pa, arrived from Tibet. With several faithful lamas and lama-artists, the high priest traveled through Sikkim, India, Nepal, Ladak, everywhere erecting images of the Blessed Maitreya and teaching about Shambhala.

When the high priest with his numerous attendants visited Talai-Pho-Brang, our home in Darjeeling, he first of all paid attention to the image of Rigden Jyepo, the Ruler of Shambhala, and said:

"I see you know that the time of Shambhala has approached. The nearest path for attainment now is only through Rigden Jyepo. If you know the Teaching of Shambhala—you know the future."

During his successive visits to us, the High Priest spoke more than once of Kalachakra, attributing to this teaching not only a religious meaning, but applying it to Life, as a real Yoga.

One may meet the teaching of Kalachakra for the first time in 1027 of our era, when it was spread by Atisha. This is the Yoga of utilizing the high energies. From ancient times, in a few monasteries—the more learned ones—special schools of Shambhala have been established. Tashi-Lhunpo was always the chief center of the vital Yoga, because the Tashi-Lamas have been the high protectors of Kalachakra and were closely linked with Shambhala. In Lhasa, Moruling is considered one of the most advanced monasteries practicing Kalachakra; this monastery has only about three hundred lamas. It is said that from time to time the most learned of these lamas go to a mysterious retreat in the Himalayas and some of them never return. In some other monasteries of Geluk-pa, the yellow sect, the teaching of Kalachakra is also practiced. This is also the case at Kumbum, the native site of Tsong-Kha-Pa, and in the Chinese monastery of Wu-tai-Shan, the high priest of which has written a remarkable book, "The Red Path to Shambhala," which is not yet translated.

In Chumbi monastery is preserved a huge banner, representing the spiritual battle of Rigden Jyepo. In this composition one sees legions of faithful warriors from all parts of the world, hastening to take part in the great conflict for spiritual victory.

When our attention is fixed on a subject, like a light which penetrates dark corners, more and more details emerge.

Not long ago, in the "Shanghai Times," and subsequently in many other newspapers, an extensive article appeared signed by Dr. Lao-Tsin, telling of his journey to the Valley of Shambhala. In a vital narrative, Dr. Lao-Tsin tells many details of his difficult journey with a Nepalese Yogi through Mongolian deserts and severe uplands to the Valley, where he found an abode of numerous Yogis studying the High Wisdom. His description of the laboratories, temples and also of the famous tower, are surprisingly analogous to the descriptions of the remarkable place in other sources. He told of many scientific wonders and of complex experiments in will power and telepathy, conducted over very great distances. It was significant to see how many countries were interested in his information.

When we traveled through the Sikkim monasteries we met several learned lamas who, although of the Red Sect, more than once mentioned the great approaching era and many details of Shambhala.

A learned lama, pointing down the slopes of the mountain, said:

"Down below, near the stream, is a remarkable cave,

but the descent to it is very difficult. In Kandro Sampo, a cave not far from Tashi-ding beside a hot spring, dwelt Padma Sambhava himself. A certain giant, planning to penetrate across Tibet, attempted to build a passage into the Sacred Land. The Blessed Teacher rose up, and growing great in height, struck the bold adventurer. Thus was destroyed the giant. And now the image of Padma Sambhava is in the cave and behind it is a stone door. It is known that behind this door the Teacher hid secret mysteries for the future. But the dates for their revelation have not yet come."

Another lama said:

"There is a legend taken from an ancient Tibetan book, wherein, under symbols, are given the future movement of the Dalai-Lama and Tashi-Lama, which already have been fulfilled. There are described the special physical marks of Rulers, under whom the country shall fall. But after, the rule shall be regained and then Someone of greatness will come. His coming is calculated in twelve years—which will be in 1936."

At dusk, a Gelong said of the Lord Maitreya:

"A man searched for twelve years for Maitreya Buddha. Nowhere did he find Him and, angered, he rejected his faith. As he continued his way, he beheld one who with a horse hair was sawing an iron rod, repeating to himself, 'If the whole of life will not be enough, yet I will saw this through.' Confusion fell on the wanderer. 'What mean my twelve years,' he said, 'in the face of such persistence? I shall return to my search.'

"Thereupon, before the man appeared Maitreya Buddha Himself and said: 'Long have I been with thee, but thou didst not see me, didst repulse me and spit upon me. I shall perform a test. Go to the bazaar. I shall be upon thy shoulder.' The man went, aware that he carried the God. But the men around him shrunk from him, closing their noses and eyes. 'Wherefore do you shrink from me, people?' he asked. 'What a fright you have on your shoulders—an ill-smelling dog full of boils,' they replied.

"Again the people did not see Maitreya Buddha, for they beheld only what each was worthy of seeing."

* * *

Sensitive are the souls here. Your emotions and desires are being transmitted so easily. Therefore, know clearly what you desire. Otherwise, instead of God, you shall behold the dog.

The old high priest of a monastery said: "Our temple is very old. For many years I used to rest in the temple each night, ending and beginning the day with prayers. Once at night, I was awakened. Before me I saw two women dressed in Tibetan garments. They bade me leave the temple at once and, taking me under my arms, led me to the steps of the entrance, where they both disappeared. At the same moment the wall of the temple crashed down and the place where I slept was crushed to pieces. Thus, two blessed Taras saved my humble life. And in their solicitude for me, they assumed the appearance of Tibetan women in order not to frighten me with their sudden appearance at night. The time of Shambhala is coming and many wonderful signs will appear before the Great Advent."

The old priest knew of other wonderful things. Like the hermit Milaraspa, he had heard inaudible voices. He had heard the flight of invisible birds and bees. Just on that day, he had had a vision before dawn, when many flames leaped up like a garland on the mountain slope. These fiery signs accompany the era of Shambhala. I repeat this as I heard it on the very scene of the vision. We must not wonder at these unfamiliar experiences. We must know things as they now exist in many countries.

From the following episode, which we experienced, one may see how deeply the local feelings must be understood. Mrs. Roerich wanted an old image of Buddha. But this is not easy, because old images are very rare and the owners have no intention to part with them. We spoke about it only among ourselves. To our surprise, some days later a lama came to see us and with a bow took out a beautiful Tibetan image of Lord Buddha from his coat and presented it to Mrs. Roerich, saying: "Memsahib wanted to have an image of Buddha. The Blessed White Tara appeared to me in a dream and ordered me to give you this image of the Blessed One, from my altar." In this way we receive a long-desired image.

Another unforgettable incident occurred near Ghum Monastery. One day, about noon, four of us were motoring on the mountain road. Suddenly our driver slowed down. On the narrow road we saw a porte-chaise, borne by four men in gray. In the porte-chaise was seated a lama, with long black hair and with a small black beard which is quite unusual for lamas. On his head he wore a crown. His red and yellow vestment was sparklingly clean. The porte-chaise passed close to us and the lama smilingly nodded several times. We continued our way, retaining our impression of the unusual lama for a long time after. Later we tried to find him, but to our great astonishment, the local lamas informed us, that in the entire district there was no such lama. They also told us that in porte-chaises none but the Dalai-Lama, the Tashi-Lama and the dead of high ranks are carried, that the crown is used only in the temple. The lamas whispered: "Probably you saw a lama from Shambhala!"

One Tibetan lama, during his visit to the holy places of India, met an old Hindu sadhu, who did not understand Tibetan, in the train. By chance the lama began to speak to him. Although the latter answered him in Hindustani, both understood each other. When the lama told us of this experience, he added:

"Only in the time of Shambhala shall all languages be understood without previous study. Because we hear and understand not the outward sound; and we see not through the physical eye, but through the third eye, which you see symbolized on the forehead of our images—this is the eye of Brahma, the eye of all-seeing knowledge. In the time of Shambhala, we will not need to rely only on our physical sight. We shall be able to evoke our great inner forces."

On the summits of Sikkim, the foothills of the Himalayas, among the blooming rhododendrons and inhaling the fragrant Balu—the healing plant—a lama, looking like a carved image of the middle ages pointing towards the five summits of Kinchenjunga, told us:

"There is the entrance to the holy land of Shambhala. By passages through wonderful ice-caves under the earth, a few deserving ones, even in this life have reached the holy place, where all wisdom, all glory, all splendor are gathered."

Another lama of the Red Sect told us about wonderful Asaras, seemingly Hindu, with long hair and white attire who often appear in the Himalayas, "the wise men who know how to master the inner energies and to unite them with cosmic energies." According to the lama, the head of the Medical School in Lhasa, a learned old lama, knew such Asaras personally and was in personal touch with them.

The "Statesman," the most precise newspaper of India, published the following experience related by a British major: "Once before sunrise while camping in the Himalayas, the major went from his camp to the neighboring cliffs to see the majestic snow-capped outlines of the mountains. On the opposite side of the gorge rose a high rock. Great was his astonishment when through the morning mist he noticed on the rock the figure of a tall man, almost naked and with long black hair. The man was leaning on a high bow, attentively watching something behind the rock. Then, apparently noticing something, the silent figure, with great strides, leaped down the almost vertical slope. Completely amazed, the major returned to the camp and asked the servants about this strange apparition. But to his utter surprise, they took it quite calmly and with reverence told him:

" 'Sahib has seen one of the snowmen, who guard the forbidden region.' "

We asked a lama about the snowmen and again the answer came in a surprisingly calm and affirmative way:

"These snowmen are very rarely seen. They are the faithful guardians of the Himalaya regions, where the secret Ashrams of the Mahatmas are hidden. Formerly even in Sikkim we had several Ashrams of the Mahatmas. These wise Mahatmas of the Himalayas direct our lives through unceasing work and study. They master the highest powers. As ordinary people, they appear in various places, here, beyond the ocean and throughout Asia."

To our surprise, our friend mentioned a story, which we had already heard, of how one of the Mahatmas, for some urgent reason, undertook a hasty journey to Mongolia, remaining in the saddle about sixty hours.

* * *

One experiences a special emotion in these remote mountains, on discovering the living words of that which he has read in the pages of distant books, because the white surfaces of glaciers often conceal the physical traces of travelers. But a simple disinterested narrative conveys a highly realistic feeling.

Truly, many things, which are seemingly fantastic and fairy-like, when observed without prejudice on the very places of their occurrence, become transmuted into a living force. And the majestic images of the Mahatmas no longer pass before our eyes as phantoms; they become great physical beings, true Masters of the Higher Knowledge and Power.

You may ask me why, in speaking of Shambhala, I mention the Great Mahatmas. Your question would be justified because, until now these two great conceptions have been separated in literature due to lack of information. But after studying the writings about the Great Mahatmas and after learning of Shambhala here, it is highly significant to see the links between these two concepts and finally to understand how near they are one to another in reality.

In Hindu literature, in the Vishnu Puranas, you may find several indications, which are understood equally by students of the Teaching of the Mahatmas and by the faithful devotees of the Teaching of Shambhala.

In the old scriptures, there are inspiring indications about a new era, about great avatars coming to save humanity, about the sacred city Kalapa, about the efforts of the Arhats in every century to arouse the slumbering spirit of humanity. We see the same indications in the Teachings of the Great Mahatmas, and in the scriptures and sagas concerning Shambhala. In

Sanskrit, in Hindustani, in Chinese, in Turki, in the Kalmuck, Mongolian and Tibetan languages, and in many minor Asiatic tongues the same ideas, the same indications concerning the Future are expressed.

One might perhaps attribute this to the usual Messianic idea. One might even believe that in the ancient period of the Nestorians and Manicheans, scattered through Asia for several centuries the concepts of a second Advent were transformed into this teaching of the future. Perhaps it seems so from afar. But studying the subject at its source, among the various nationalities who are separated by immense deserts and many thousands of miles, you see that these teachings are far more ancient than the Messianic idea and they deal not only with a personification, but mostly with the conception of a new era, identified with gigantic cosmic energies.

In the basic teaching of Buddha one may already find some suggestions about a future attainment of humanity. Under the symbol of an iron serpent encircling the earth and transporting and laboring for humanity, you see the symbols of railways. Under the symbol of flying iron birds, you understand aircrafts. In indications about life on the stars and in the allusions to the various states of human existence, you may recognize the same problems which science is gradually confirming—of life on the planets, of the discoveries of the astral world, all of which but recently ceased to be subjects for ridicule.

It is truly strange to recognize links between the

oldest Vedic traditions and the new conceptions of Einstein. But we must not forget that even Buddha came to clarify the declining and corrupted forms of culture and taught about the subtle Cosmic Energies. Only recently in the districts of Karachi and Lahore, were found ruins of ancient cities, 5000 to 6000 years old, showing the advanced culture of ancient India. This culture reminds one of the culture of the Sumerians and Elams. Many cylinders like those of Babylon were found in these ruins, disclosing a new literature when deciphered. Without these comparatively recent discoveries, India's medieval glory would seem to have ended only several centuries before our era. The words of the ancient legends and scriptures came as if from the unknown space; but these discoveries have now given a basis of reality to this ancient knowledge. In the light of these wayside stones, we may begin to think about the indications of Plato, about the destruction of Poseidon, the last stronghold of Atlantis.

Thus, we see that many symbols and signs are in fact far more ancient than the age attributed to them by science of the last century.

Many concepts which would seem to be completely unrelated reveal a close connection, upon attentive and unprejudiced study.

For instance, what connection has Buddhism with early Christianity? But even Origen refers to the Buddhists and Druids of Britain. The missionaries of King Ashoka might easily have gone to Britain and come into contact with the old sun cult of the Druids. The serpent lore of Scotland must be considered parallel with the dragon lore of China, as well as with the serpent lore of India. The great sign of the cross is universal and traverses all ages, through Egypt, the Svastika of untold antiquity.

One listens with special emotion to the old prophecies and legends, which represent to these learned lamas and Brahmins the real wisdom and the Teaching of Life.

In order to convey a sense of this atmosphere, I shall give extracts from the Vishnu Puranas and translations from Tibetan Prophecies.

Among the commandments of Tsong-Kha-Pa, there is one that indicates that the Arhats each century attempt to enlighten the world. Up to the present, none of these attempts has been successful. It is said that until Panchen Rinpoche (the Tashi-Lama) consents to be reborn in the land of the Pelings (Westerners) and, as the spiritual conqueror, to destroy the age-old errors and ignorance, it will be of little use to try to uproot the misconceptions of the Pelings.

In 1924, Alexandra David-Neal, who had been in Tibet, wrote several articles about the traditions of Gessar Khan, whose legendary personality stands besides Rigden Jyepo, Ruler of Shambhala, and has many links with him.

She brought back the ancient prophecies about Gessar Khan, of how he gathers his faithful warriors and goes to purge Lhasa of its nefarious elements.

In her article, "The Coming Northern Hero," Mrs. David-Neal says: "Gessar Khan is a hero, whose new incarnation will take place in Northern Shambhala. There he will unite his co-workers and leaders, who have followed him in his previous life. They also will incarnate in Shambhala, whereto they will be attracted by the mysterious power of their Ruler or by the mysterious voices, which are heard only by the initiate." The Ruler Gessar Khan is coming with an invincible army, to destroy the nefarious elements of Lhasa and to establish justice and prosperity everywhere.

In Tibet we had occasion to convince ourselves of this legend. We were told of Gessar Khan's palace in Kham, where the swords of his army are collected, serving as beams for his palace. The arrow is the sign of Gessar Khan. His arrows are lightning and the arrow-tips found in fields are considered to be crystallized thunderbolts. War is declared by the shooting of an arrow. The order for mobilization is, as we have seen, wrapped around an arrow. Gessar Khan is armed with arrows of thunder and the predestined army is soon ready to come out of the sacred land for the salvation of mankind. He who can read the sacred runes will understand to what new epoch of spiritual triumph these symbols refer.

* * *

Let us recall also the Tibetan prophecies about Shambhala and Maitreya:

PROPHECIES OF SHAMBHALA AND MAITREYA

The Treasure is returning from the West. On the Mountains the fires of Jubilation are kindled.

There walk those who carry the Stone. Upon the Shrine are the signs of Maitreya. Out of the Sacred Kingdom is given the date when the carpet of expectation may be spread. By the signs of the seven stars shall the Gates be opened.

By Fire shall I manifest My Messengers.

Gather the prophecies of your happiness.

* * *

Thus are the prophecies of the ancestors fulfilled and the writings of the wise ones. Gather thy understanding to hail the Predestined.

When in the fifth Year the heralds of the warriors of Northern Shambhala shall appear, gather understanding to meet them. And receive the New Glory! I shall manifest My Sign of Lightning.

* * *

THE COMMAND OF GESSAR KHAN

I have many treasures but only upon the appointed day may I bestow them upon My People. When the legions of Northern Shambhala shall bring the Spear of Salvation, then shall I uncover the depths of the mountain and you will divide among the warriors and yourselves equally My Treasures. And live in justice.

The time shall soon come for that command of Mine

to cross all deserts. When My gold was scattered by the winds, I ordained the day when the people of Northern Shambhala would come to gather My possessions. Then shall My people prepare their sacks for the treasures. And to each shall I give a just share.

* * *

One may find sands of gold. One may find precious gems. But the true wealth shall come only with the People of Northern Shambhala. When the time is come to send them forth.

Thus is ordained.

* * *

It is predicted that the manifestations of Maitreya shall come after the wars. But the final war shall be for the cause of the True Teaching. But each one rising up against Shambhala, shall be stricken in all his works. And the waves shall wash away his dwellings.

And even a dog shall not answer to his call. Not clouds but lightning shall he see on the final night.

And the fiery messenger shall rise up on pillars of Light. The teaching indicates that each warrior of Shambhala shall be named the Invincible.

The Lord Himself hastens. And His Banner is already above the mountains.

* * *

Thy Pastures shall reach the Promised Land.

When thou tendest thy flocks, dost thou not hear the voices of the stones? These are the toilers of Maitreya, who make ready for thee the treasures.

When the wind murmurs through the reeds, dost thou understand that these are the arrows of Maitreya, flying in protection?

When lightning illumines your camps, knowest thou that this is the light of the desired Maitreya?

To whom shall be entrusted the watch upon the first night—to thee. To whom shall My envoy be dispatched —to thee. Who shall meet them—thou.

From the West, from the mountains, shall come My People. Who shall receive and safe-guard them—thou.

Beseech the Tara to rest with thee. Will, to cleanse thy hearts until My Coming.

Each one hearing My desires, shall cover his fur-cap with a fiery cover and shall entwine the head-strap of his horse with a fiery cord.

Look sharply upon the rings of the coming ones. There where is My chalice—there is thy salvation. Upon the mountain, fires are kindled.

Coming is the New Year. Whoever shall out-slumber it shall not again awaken. Northern Shambhala is come!

We know not fear. We know not depression. Dukkar, the many-eyed and many-armed, sends us pure thoughts. Ponder with pure thoughts. Ponder with thoughts of light.

* * *

One-two-three! I see three peoples.

One-two-three! I see three books. The first is of the Blessed One Himself. The second is given by Asvagosha. The third is given by Tsong-Kha-Pa.

One-two-three! I see three books of the coming of Maitreya. The first is written in the West. The second is written in the East. The third is written in the North.

One-two-three! I see three manifestations. The first is with the sword. The second is with the law. The third is with the light.

One-two-three! I see three horses. The first is black. The second is red. The third is white.

One-two-three! I see three ships. The first is on the waters. The second is under the waters. The third is above the earth.

One-two-three! I see three eagles. The first is perched upon the stone. The second is pecking at his prey. The third is flying towards the sun.

One-two-three! I see the seekers of light. Red ray! Blue ray! Ray of silvery-white!

* * *

I affirm that the Teaching issued from Bodh-Gaya and shall return there. When the procession carrying the Image of Shambhala shall pass through the lands of Buddha and return to the first source, then shall arrive the time of the pronunciation of the sacred word of Shambhala.

Then shall one receive merit from the pronouncement of this name.

Then shall the thought of Shambhala provide sustenance. Then shall affirmation of Shambhala become the beginning of all works and gratitude to Shambhala their end. And great and small shall be filled with understanding of the Teaching.

Sacred Shambhala is pictured amidst the swords and spears, in impenetrable armor.

Solemnly I affirm: Shambhala the invincible!

Fulfilled is the circle of the bearing of the Image! In the sites of Buddha; in the sites of Maitreya, is brought the image. Pronounced is "Kalagiya" as the banner of the Image unfurls.

What has been pronounced is as true as that under the Stone of Ghum lies the Prophecy of Sacred Shambhala.

The Banner of Shambhala shall encircle the central lands of the Blessed Ones. Those who accept Him shall rejoice. And those who deny Him shall tremble.

The Tashi-Lama shall ask the Great Dalai-Lama: "What is predestined for the last Dalai-Lama?"

He who denies shall be given over to justice and shall be forgotten. And the warriors shall march under the banner of Maitreya. And the city of Lhasa shall be obscured and deserted.

Those rising against Shambhala shall be cast down. To those in darkness, the Banner of Maitreya shall flow as blood, over the lands of the new world. To those who have understood, as a red sun.

The Tashi-Lama shall find the Great Dalai-Lama and the Great Dalai-Lama shall thus address him: "I will send thee the worthiest sign of my lightning. Go, overtake Tibet. The ring shall protect thee."

Let us also remember some Hindu traditions:

The Kalki Purana thus mentions the Kalki Avatar, that is yet to come:

"At your request I shall take birth in the abode of Shambhala. I shall again place the two rulers, Maru and Devapi, on earth. I shall create Satya-Yuga and restore the Dharma to its former condition and after destroying the serpent Kali, I shall return to my own abode."

Vishnu Purana continues:

"Devapi and Maru . . . dwelling in Kalapa and endowed with great yogic powers, guided by Vasudeva, at the end of Kali will establish Varna and Ashrama Dharma as before."

Shrimad Bhagavata in book VI says:

"These Maharishis and other great Sidhas are moving about on the face of the earth for the purpose of affording spiritual enlightenment to those who follow worldly attractions; thus do I."

Shankaracharya, in his Viveka Chudamani says:

"Those Great Ones, who have attained peace and have Themselves finished swimming across the fearful ocean of births and deaths, exist and move for the good of the people, as does the Spring. Unselfishly they liberate mankind."

The Vishnu Purana speaks of the end of Kali-Yuga, when barbarians will be masters of the banks of the Indus:

"There will be temporal monarchs, reigning over the earth, kings of churlish spirit, violent temper and addicted to constant falsehood and cruelty. They will inflict death on women and children and they will seize upon the property of their subject . . . their lives will be short, their desires insatiable. People of various countries will intermingle with them. Wealth will decrease, until the world will be wholly demoralized.

"Property alone will confer rank; wealth will be the only source of devotion. Passion will be the sole bond between sexes. Perjury will be the only means of success in litigation. Women will be objects merely of sensual gratification. A rich man will be reputed pure. Fine attire will be the mark of dignity.

"Thus in the Kali age, will decay continue. Then at the end of the Kali Yuga, the Kalki Avatar shall descend upon earth. He will reëstablish righteousness. When the Sun and Moon and Tishya and the planet Jupiter are in one mansion, the Satya Age will return—the white age!"

Thus say the Agni Puranas:

"At the end of Kali Yuga there will be mixed castes. Robbers will be numerous. Under cover of religion, men will preach irreligion. And the Mlechhas, in the guise of kings, will devour men. Armed with a coat of mail and weapons, Vishnuyasha's son Kalki, will annihilate the Mlechhas, establish order and dignity and lead the people on the path of truth. Then, having renounced the form of Kalki, Hari will return to heaven.

"Thereupon Kritayuga will exist as before."

* * *

With a pilgrim's staff let us pass through Benares, where it is said that Maitreya will be born. Let us cross the old road to Kadarnath, leading to the great Kailas, abode of mighty hermits and the milestone to Shambhala. Let us pass Lahore, with its old neighboring cities. Let us go to Kashmir and the throne of Solomon on the summit of the mountain. There, in the land of Ashoka's son, stood a Buddhist temple, destroyed by the Hindus. In these ancient places once again is heard the name of Maitreya.

Reaching the Ladak border in Dras, besides old Neolithic designs, you may see the first image of Maitreya on the rocks. Thus again, both the signs of the future—the Great Rider, the Kalki Avatar of India and the Maitreya predestined by Buddhism, stand on the same road, blessing the pilgrims.

In ancient Maulbeck, where several ruined monasteries recall the beautiful past, we were greeted on a most ancient road by a majestic image of Maitreya, probably carved by an Indian hand and bearing a Chinese inscription. Is it not the same significant image which Fa-hsien, the renowned Chinese traveler so reverently describes, in his memoirs?

Even in Lamayuru, the old citadel of the Bon-po, this impenetrable half-Shaman religion, we found to our great surprise an image of Maitreya. It seemed strange that a Bon-po temple, which rejects even Buddha, should be concerned with Maitreya, the Lord of the Future, predestined by Buddha. And yet this call of the future penetrates the places which are hostile even to Buddha Himself.

In Saspul, a more ancient image, probably from the

sixth century, exists. An old lama, showing us this relic, whispered to us of the approaching New Era. In this small village with its many ruins dotting the summit of the mountains, it was strange to hear about a brilliant future. But this devotion to the future lends to these isolated places not only a sense of the past, but the sense of milestones, for achievements already predestined. If you show the old lama that you comprehend his language not only literally, but in its inner meaning, he will tell you many remarkable indications. If you show him some prophecies received in India or Sikkim, mark with what keen interest he will ask you for permission to copy them. Be sure he will not keep them for himself alone, but traveling lamas will carry these signs of a regeneration to other isolated places.

Like a stronghold, high on the mountains, is one of the oldest monasteries, the Spithug monastery.

The high lama of this monastery was doubtful as to how to greet us or in what way to address us, so that the first moments of our visit here were somewhat delicate. But when we spoke of the concept of Shambhala, the front door was widely opened. We were invited into the picturesque room of the Incarnate Lama, surprisingly clean and inviting. Instead of a superficial conversation, we were at once asked how we knew of Shambhala; again many new details were told us and we saw that our host really regretted it when the time for our leave-taking came. "Someone from the West—and knowing of Shambhala! This is a sign of the New Era!" he exclaimed.

In Leh, the capital of Ladak, are especially collected many memories of Gessar Khan and Shambhala. Ladak is regarded as the birth place of Gessar Khan. The Maharaja of Ladak is said to be a descendant of Gessar Khan. Many beautiful and romantic legends and songs dedicated to the great hero, Gessar Khan, and his wife Bruguma, are related and sung in Ladak. Here, high on the rocks, you may see a white door leading to the castles of Gessar Khan. Here, also, on a rock, is the image of a huge lion, connected with the same hero. On the roads, several images of Maitreya may be seen. In Leh, near the temple of Buddha and of Dukkar, the Mother of the World, is a special temple finely decorated, dedicated to Maitreya. In the silent dusk of the temple you may distinguish on the beautifully painted walls, the figures of Bodhisattvas, and in the two-storied center, ready to descend from His throne, is the image of the Lord Maitreya. This temple is ornamented with special veneration—the same veneration you feel when lamas come to your home to see the images of the Lord Maitreya and Shambhala.

One of our Western friends, unfamiliar with Buddhistic matters, on observing the Tanka of Shambhala, remarked that it seemed like the usual Tibetan banner. I asked him where and how often he had seen the same subject. Whereupon he naïvely admitted, "Well, perhaps not identically this one; but also with some Buddhas."

After realizing the great subtlety of Eastern symbology and Buddhist ikonography, it is strange to hear such superficial remarks about "some Buddhas." One may imagine the impression that such a "gentleman of some Buddhas" makes in an Eastern temple, where he speaks so lightly of such revered images. For some, everyone who sits cross-legged is a Buddha. Through such ignorance, deep misunderstandings are created.

One of the educated Buddhists told us how he saved three Germans, who entered the temple smoking. Immediately, the crowd, peaceful until that moment, became furious and threatened bloodshed.

Not only should we not violate the feeling of people of different religions, but we should feel that the study of the subject in itself expands our outlook on life and gives real joy of knowledge.

Let us remember some Ladaki songs on religious subjects:

Just before approaching the severe Sasser and Karakorum passes, for the last time, we saw the image of Lord Maitreya in the frontier monastery of Sandoling. This monastery is renowned because there is a rock behind the monastery on which the rays of the setting sun project wonderful images. This is an old monastery somewhat deteriorated externally. It was, therefore, more surprising to find absolutely new images of the Lord Maitreya, Shambhala and Dukkar there. In this way, we should remember where the modern creative thought is directed.

During many days of travel through no-man's-land, we saw no milestones, no trace of a religious life. But facing the glaciers we were reminded several times of the great names of the Future.

In the late evening, just before crossing rocky Kurul Davan, an unexpected guest visited us, an old gray-bearded Moslem. Surrounded by huge rocks before the tent, in the moonlight, we spoke about the Koran and Mahomet. He told us how Mahomet venerated womanhood. Then he spoke about the manuscripts and legends of Issa, (Jesus) the best of human sons. He told us how Moslems are eager to obtain everything concerning Issa at any cost.

Then we spoke of Muntazar, the Moslem symbol corresponding to the Kalki Avatar of the Hindus and to Maitreya of the Buddhists. Our unexpected friend became enthusiastic. And on his lips the name of Maitreya was uttered with the same veneration as that of Muntazar. In his hopes, one felt the future world unity, the future joy and understanding.

After crossing four snowy passes, when we were already in the desert itself, we again saw a picture of the future. In a spot surrounded by sharp, cragged rocks, three caravans had stopped for the night. At sunset I witnessed a unique episode. On one of the stones a colorful Tibetan banner had been placed. Several people sat before it in reverent silence. A lama in red robes and a yellow cap, with a stick was pointing out something to them on this painting, and rhythmically chanted a descriptive prayer. Approaching we saw the familiar tanka of Shambhala. The lama was chanting about the innumerable treasures of the King of Shambhala and about his miraculous ring bestowed on him by the Highest Powers. Designating with his pointer the battle of Rigden Jyepo, the lama related how all evil beings shall perish mercilessly before the righteous force of the Ruler.

The camp fires glowed—the fire flies of the desert! Again from many countries, people gathered round one fire. Ten fingers were raised in awe as they related ecstatically how Blessed Rigden Jyepo reveals Himself to give commands to His messengers. Perhaps how on the black rock of Ladak the mighty Ruler appears, and from all directions the mounted messengers with deep obeisance approach to hearken; how at full speed they hasten to fulfill what is ordained by His great wisdom.

* * *

In Ladak for the first time we met a remarkable custom practiced by the lamas. During storms they ascend a mountain peak and in prayer, cast to the wind tiny images of horses. These are sent to help travelers in distress. One could not help recalling the legend of the North Dvina River, which tells how St. Procopius the Righteous, sitting on the high banks of the mighty river, prayed for unknown travelers. Such signs of pan-human love!

Descending the mountains to the sands of Taklamakan, where you meet only Moslems, Sarts and Chinese and where you see the mosques and Chinese temples of Khotan, one would not expect to see anything about Shambhala. And yet, just there we again came upon valuable information. Not far from Khotan, are many ruins of old Buddhist temples and stupas. One of these stupas is identified with the legend, that in the time of Shambhala, a mysterious light will shine from it. It is said that this light has already been seen.

Many Kalmucks from Karashahr visit this place in worship. It is also said that the Lord Buddha passed these places during his journey to the far North, to Altai.

During our stay in Yarkend, Kashgar and Kuchar, the people told us that in Kashgar there lived a holy man who at sunrise heard the cocks crow in the distant holy land, which was six months' journey away.

Between Maral Bashi and Kuchar our sais, Suleiman, pointing at a mountain to the south-east, said:

"There, behind that mountain, live holy men. They have departed from the world in order to save humanity through their wisdom. Many have tried to reach their land, but few have ever reached it. They know that one must go beyond that mountain. But as soon as they have crossed the ridge, they lose their way."

One may easily perceive that these legends refer to Shambhala and that even the geographical indications in them point in the same direction as the Shambhala of all Nations.

* * *

After passing the Moslem cities and deserted cave temples of the old Tokhar districts, we reached Karashahr, where Buddhism flourishes even now.

Karashahr is not only a stronghold of the Karashahr

Kalmucks but also the last resting place of the Chalice of Buddha, as cited by the historians. The Chalice of the Blessed One was brought here from Peshawar and disappeared here. As is said, "The Chalice of Buddha will be found again, when the time of Shambhala will approach."

Purushapura, or Peshawar, for long was the City of the Chalice of Buddha. After the death of the Teacher, the Chalice was brought to Peshawar where it remained for long the object of deep reverence. During the time of the Chinese traveler, Fa-hsien, about 400 B. C., the Chalice was still at Peshawar, in a monastery especially built for it. It was of many colors, with black predominating and the outlines of the four chalices which composed it were clearly seen.

During the time of Hsuan-tsang, another Chinese traveler, in about 630 A. D., the Chalice was no longer at Peshawar. It was in Persia or in Karashahr already.

In the East we cannot disregard the concept of a Chalice.

The Chalice of Buddha was miraculous and inexhaustible—a true Chalice of Life.

Let us remember the chalice of Amritha and the struggle for its possession, as related so poetically in the Mahabharata. Indra takes the chalice of the King of the Nagas and carries it to heaven.

According to Persian traditions, when Jemshid began to excavate the foundation for the city of Istaker, a miraculous Chalice, Jami-Jemshid, was found. The chalice was made of turquoise and was filled with the precious nectar of Life.

The legends from the Solovetz monastery regarding the personalities of the Old Testament, mention the chalice of King Solomon:

"Great is the Chalice of Solomon, made from a precious stone. On the Chalice are inscribed three verses in the Sumerian character and no one can explain them."

The Moslems in Khandakhar have their own sacred Chalice.

In Kharran there is also a sacred chalice, Faa-Faga. From this chalice those drink who take part in the mysteries. On the seventh day they announce:

"O Teacher, may the inaudible be manifest!"

In the ceremonies of Vedism, Buddhism and Mazdeism, the sacred symbol of the Chalice of Life is utilized everywhere.

Jataka tells of the origin of the Chalice of Buddha:

"Then from the four lands, came four guardians of the world and offered chalices made of sapphire. But Buddha refused them. Again they offered four chalices made of black stone (muggavanna) and he, full of compassion for the four genii, accepted the four chalices.

"He placed one into the other and ordained:

"Let there be one!"

And the edges of the four chalices became visible as outlines. All the Chalices formed one.

The Buddha accepted food in the newly formed Chalice and having partaken of the food, he offered thanks.

Lalita Vistara, describing the sacraments of the Chalice of Buddha, attributes to the Blessed One the following significant address to the Kings who brought the chalices:

"Pay thy respect to Buddha, in the name of the Chalice, and the Chalice shalt be to thee as a vessel of knowledge.

"If thou wilt offer the Chalice to thy peers, thou wilt not remain, either in memory, nor in judgment.

"But who offers the Chalice to Buddha, will not be forgotten either in memory or wisdom."

This Chalice—the Ark of Life, the Chalice of Salvation—must be discovered soon again.

Thus they know in the deserts.

* * *

In Karashahr we met Toin Lama, the Chief Prince of the Karashahr Kalmucks. It is said of him that he is a re-incarnation of the famous Sanchen Lama of Shigatse, the Prime Minister of the Tashi-Lama. Sanchen Lama was tortured to death by the Lhasa Government because it accused him of treason for his relations with the well-known traveler Chandra Das. It is not forgotten that the old Sanchen Lama previously predicted his own fate and even ordered a painting to be made of the lake, in which he was afterwards drowned. He also predicted that he would incarnate soon again in the country of the Kalmucks and on the knee of the Toin Lama is to be seen the same characteristic mark as that of the Sanchen Lama.

With great astonishment, Toin Lama listened to us speak about Shambhala. "Verily," he said, "the great time has come if you come from the West and you know the greatest knowledge! We all are ready to sacrifice all our possessions, everything that may be of use to Shambhala. All riders will be mounted when the Blessed Rigden Jyepo will need them."

* * *

As you approach Turfan, still more legends reach you. The ancient Buddhist cave-temples, subterranean dwellings and passages, and even the old underground canals for irrigation, all this gives an unusual aspect to the place. And everything directs your thought to the same conception of distant holy countries, where dwell wise folk anxious to serve humanity. As they relate:

"From a cave came a stranger—very tall and in a strange attire. He came to the bazaar in Turfan, in order to buy some things; and in exchange he gave a golden coin for them. After, when we looked at this coin more closely, we saw that for more than a thousand years such coins had already been out of use. This man came from the holy land."

Or one says:

"Out of one of the subterranean passages came a woman, tall, serious and of darker complexion than ourselves. She went among the people to help them. She also came from the holy land." . . .

"Horsemen of a most unusual appearance were seen near a cave; then all disappeared. Probably they went through a subterranean passage to their own land. Through many of the passages one can even go on horseback."

How many are there of such unknown riders—messengers!

Nearing Zaisan our Kalmuck lama, pointing south-west to the silvery snow range, said: "Over there is our sacred Mount Sawur. From its summit one can see the mountains of the Sacred Land on clear days. Under the hill, there is the city of Ayushi Khan, covered by sand. One can still see the walls, temples and suburgans."

Wilder and wilder are the mountain ranges from Chuguchak to Altai. It is strange to see the Oirots, a Finno-Turkish tribe, secluded in the Altai mountains. Only recently, this country, with its beautiful forests and thundering streams and snow-white summits, began to be called by the name of Oirotia, land of the Blessed Oirot—the national hero of this secluded tribe.

A remarkable incident occurred in this country, where crude forms of Shamanism and sorcery were formerly practiced. About fifteen years ago, a young Oirot girl had a vision: the Blessed Oirot as a mighty rider, on a white steed, appeared and told her that he was the Messenger of the White Burkhan, whose advent was near.

The girl received from the Blessed One many commands on how to introduce righteous customs in the country and how to address the White Burkhan who would establish a new happy era on earth. The girl summoned the entire clan together and proclaimed to them the new Teaching, bidding them destroy their pagan altars and to pray to the merciful White Burkhan. On the mountain summit was founded a cult. The people gathered together, burnt juniper, and sang their newly composed songs, so elevating and touching. Upon the peaks of the mountain Cherem they thus addressed the White Burkhan:

"Thou who dwellest behind white clouds
Behind the blue skies—
Three Kurbustans!
Thou, wearing four tresses—
White Burkhan!
Thou, Spirit of Altai—
White Burkhan!

"Thou peopling within thyself, in gold and silver
A nation, White Altai!
Thou who illuminest the day—
Sun—Burkhan!
Thou who illuminest the night—
Moon—Burkhan!

"Let my call be inscribed
Into the book Sudur!"

The local government became perturbed at this new religion, as they called it. And the peaceful followers of the White Burkhan were even persecuted. But the

Blessed Oirot still rides over the Altai mountains and the Faith in the White Burkhan is growing. Through the scattered yurtas is whispered a legend, that on the Katun river the last battle of humanity will take place and that behind a distant white mountain the shining light of the White Burkhan can already be seen. At the same time the heads of the narrators turn to the south of Altai, where, far off, rise the highest mountains, brilliant in their snowy adornment. This happened in the Oirot tribe of the Altai mountains.

In the same mountains, another remarkable event connected with Shambhala and the New Era, is to be mentioned. In the same mountain district live many so-called Old Believers. Centuries ago, they fled into the dense forests, attempting to escape the persecutions against them, which started in the XVIIth Century, during Patriarch Nikon's time, and continuing with especial severity after the time of Peter the Great.

The old faith is orthodoxly kept there, even until now. They have their own ikons. They have their own priests. They use special expressions in their prayers. Even now, everything that occurs in Siberia only slightly affects this remote people.

In the middle of the XIXth Century a strange message was brought to the Altai Old Believers from somewhere:

"In distant lands, beyond the great lakes, beyond the highest mountains, is a sacred place where all truth flourishes.

"There exists the supreme knowledge and the future

salvation of mankind. And this place is called Belovodye, meaning the white waters."

In secret scriptures the road to this place is outlined. The geographical landmarks around this place are purposely misspelt in order to conceal them, or else they are incorrectly pronounced. But despite the faulty spelling, you can distinguish the correct geographical direction and this direction—to your surprise—again leads you to the Himalayas.

A serious gray-bearded Old Believer, if he becomes your friend, will say to you:

"From here, you go between the Irtysh and Argun rivers. After a hard journey, if you do not lose your way, you come to the salt lakes. This path is very dangerous! Many people have already perished on them. But if you choose the right time, you will be able to traverse these dangerous grounds. Then you arrive at the Bogogorsh mountains. From there, begins a still more dangerous path to Kokushi. After, take the path over the Ergor itself and follow it up to the snowy land. There, in the highest mountains, is a sacred valley. This is Belovodye. If your spirit is ready to reach this place through all dangers, the people of Belovodye will greet you. And if they find you worthy, perhaps they will even permit you to remain with them. But this happens very seldom. Many people have tried to reach Belovodye. Our grandfathers, Atamanoff and Artomonoff went. They disappeared for three years and reached the sacred place, but they were not allowed to stay there and had to come back. Many wonders they told about this place and of still other wonders they were not permitted to speak."

When you realize the geographical names mentioned, after correctly spelling Irtysh and Argun, you understand that the salt lakes are the lakes of Tsaidam with their dangerous passes. Bogogorsh or Bogogorye is the mountain range Burkhan Buddha. It is easy to understand that Kokushi is the range Kokushili. And Ergor of the highest upland is the cold Chantung near the Trans-Himalayas, already in view of the Eternal Snow.

This Teaching of Belovodye is even now so strong in the Altai mountains that only six years ago, a party of Old Believers started out for this sacred place. Up to now they have not returned, but when we passed the Altai in 1926, a letter was received through a native Oirot from one woman member of this party. She had written to her relatives that they had not yet reached the sacred place. But they still hoped to reach it. She could not say where they were living at the moment, but they lived well. Thus again, legend and fairy tale are interwoven with realities. These people know of Belovodye—Shambhala—and they whisper of the path to the Himalayas.

When we crossed Altai, several village school masters came to us, asking in a lowered voice—"Are you coming from India? Tell us what you know of the Mahatmas."

And with eagerness their eyes glowed and they grasped each hint from the Teachings of the Mahatmas. And they whispered:

"There are many of us and we exist solely by this Teaching"—this, in rocky mountains and in deep forests.

On the eve of our departure from Altai for Mongolia, I heard a chant sung by a gray-bearded Old Believer, as follows:

"Oh, receive me and accept me, thou silent desert—

"How can I receive Thee, a Prince,

I have no palaces and royal chambers to house Thee?"—

"But I need no palaces and royal chambers!"

And a little boy on the mountain sings:

Oh, My Beloved Master!
Why so soon hast Thou left me?
Thou hast left me an orphan,
Grieving through all my days!
Oh, thou desert, the beautiful!
Accept me in thy embrace.
Into thy chosen palace,
Peaceful and silent.
As from a serpent, I flee
From earthly fame and splendor,
From wealth and resplendent mansions—
My desert beloved, accept me!
I shall go to thy meadows.
To rejoice at many wondrous flowers.
Here to dwell my coming years.
Until the end of my days.

I recognized the old chant about Iosaph, the son of the King. It was an old religious song about Buddha, the life of the Lord, called by the title of "The Life of Iosaph—the son of the King of India." Iosaph (Iosaphat) is really the word Bodhisattva in an Arabic distortion.

Thus again, in remote mountains, subjects which lie so decidedly apart are united in dignified peaceful understanding.

A peculiar story is told of how quite recently in Kostroma a very old monk who had long ago traveled in India and in the Himalayas, died. Among his possessions was found a manuscript with much about the Mahatmas, indicating that this monk was intimately acquainted with this subject usually kept in secrecy. Thus, unexpectedly, are scattered personal experiences and authentic indications.

To return to the same source: an old man leads us to a stony hill and solemnly pointing at the stone circles of ancient tombs, says:

"Here, the Chud went under the earth. When the White Tzar came to Altai and when the white birch tree began to bloom in our region, the Chud were unwilling to remain under the White Tzar. They went underground and closed the passage, with mighty stones. There you can see it. But the Chud did not pass forever. A new era will come, when the people from Belovodye will return and will give to the people a new knowledge, then the Chud will return with all their acquired treasures."

In Buriatia and in Mongolia we were not astonished to find many signs about Shambhala. In these countries psychic powers are rather developed. When we approached Urga, the capital of Mongolia, we had to pass one night at Iro. In the evening, across the river, we noticed a fire. We asked what it was, and received quite an unusual answer:

"There is a big monastery and just now this monastery is the subject of widespread rumors throughout Mongolia. Last year near this monastery a wonderful child was born. When it was one year old, it pronounced clearly in Mongolian an important prophecy about the future. Afterwards it never spoke again and became the usual ordinary child."

Again a message about the future!

When we entered Urga, we saw an open place near a temple, surrounded by a stockade, so usual for Mongolian dwellings.

"What is this?" we asked.

Again came a surprising reply:

"This is a site for a temple of Shambhala. An unknown lama came and purchased this place for a future building."

In Mongolia not only do many learned lamas know about Shambhala, but even many laymen and members of the Government tell you the most striking details.

When we showed some of the prophecies about Shambhala to a member of the Mongolian Government, he exclaimed in deep surprise:

"But this is the prophecy which was foretold by the

boy on the Iro river: Verily the Great Time is coming!"

And he told us how a young Mongolian lama in the region of Uliasutai quite recently wrote a new book about Shambhala, explaining the exalted meaning of Shambhala for the future, and speaking about the path to this wonderful place.

Another highly intelligent Buriat, one of the Mongolian leaders, told us how a Buriat lama reached Shambhala after many difficulties and remained there a short time. In the account of his unusual travels are some strikingly realistic details. It is told that when this lama with his guide reached the very frontier of the sacred valley, they saw a caravan of yaks with salt quite near. They were the regular Tibetan merchants and without knowing anything, they passed quite near the wonderful site. Even the air round this place is so strongly psychologized that the people cannot see anything which should not be seen.

Another detail is also striking: As this lama, returning home from Shambhala, passed a very narrow subterranean passage, he met two men carrying, with utmost difficulties, a thoroughbred sheep needed for some scientific experiments, which are being made in this remarkable valley.

In the streets of Urga one may meet a cavalry detachment of Mongolian troops, singing with specially deep emotion, a ringing song.

"What song is it?" we ask.

"This is a song about Shambhala!"

And they tell us, how Sukhe-Bator, the national hero

of Mongolia and a leader in the recent movement for freedom, composed this song about Shambhala, sung at present in all corners of Khalkha.

It begins thus:

"Chang Shambalin Dayin,
The War of Northern Shambhala!
Let us die in this war
To be reborn again
as Knights of the Ruler of Shambhala!"

Thus the latest movement in Mongolia is also combined with the name of Shambhala. And new banners are raised in honor of Shambhala.

We visited a special temple dedicated to Maitreya, and another temple of Kalachakra. There we saw an unusual tanka, showing the imaginary site of Shambhala.

When I presented my painting, representing Rigden Jyepo, the Ruler of Shambhala, to the Mongolian Government, it was accepted with marked emotions and a member of the Government told me that they wished to build a special memorial temple in which this painting would occupy the central altar.

One of the members of the Government said to me: "May I ask you how you knew the vision, which one of our most revered lamas had several months ago?" "The lama saw a great crowd of people of many nations; all of them were looking towards the West. Then in the sky, there appeared a giant rider on a fiery steed, encircled by flames, with the banner of Shambhala in his hand—the Blessed Rigden Jyepo Himself. And He Himself bid the crowd turn from the West to the East. In the description of the lama the majestic rider looked exactly as on your painting."

Such coincidences as the painting and also the prophecies on the Iro river provoked the exclamation:

"Verily the time of Shambhala has come!"

Many other similar wonders were related to us by educated Buriats and Mongols. They spoke about a mysterious light which shines above the Khotan stupa; about the coming re-appearance of the lost Chalice of Buddha. They also spoke of the miraculous stone from a distant star, which is appearing in different localities before the Great Advent. The Great Timur, it is said, temporarily possessed this stone. The stone is usually brought by completely unsuspected strangers. In the same way, at certain times, it has disappeared to be again discovered some time later in an entirely different country. The greater portion of this stone remains in Shambhala, while part of it is circulating throughout the Earth, retaining its magnetic link with the main Stone.

Endless stories are told about this Stone. King Solomon and the Emperor Akbar also are said to have possessed it. These sagas involuntarily remind one of the Lapis Exilis, sung by the famous Meistersinger Wolfram von Eschenbach, who ends this song with the line:

"Und dieser Stein ist Gral genannt!"

And this stone is named the Grail!

In Urga also we heard from several sources about the visit of the Great Mahatma Himself, the Blessed Rigden Jyepo to two of the oldest Mongolian monasteries; one, Erdeni-Dzu on the Orkhon river, and the other Narabanchi.

Of the visit of the Mahatmas to Narabanchi we had already read in literature. But we were glad to see that the same details were also told by the lamas in remote Mongolia. We were told how one night, about midnight, a group of riders approached the gates of Narabanchi Gompa. They apparently came from a distance. Their faces were covered with fur. Their Leader entered the Gompa and at once all lamps lit by themselves. Then he ordered that all the gelongs and havarags of the monastery should be called together. Approaching the Bogdogegen's seat, he uncovered his face and every one present recognized the Blessed One Himself. He pronounced prophecies of the future, after which all mounted their horses and departed as speedily as they had come.

Another story about the arrival of the Mahatma of the Himalayas to Mongolia, was told to us by a member of the Mongolian Scientific Committee.

"As you know," he told us, "we have several lamas with great spiritual powers. Naturally they do not live in cities or big monasteries but usually in remote khutons in mountain retreats. About fifty or sixty years ago, one of these lamas was entrusted with a mission. He was to carry it out alone, but before his death he was to entrust it to one person of his own choice. You know that the greatest missions are assigned from Shambhala, but on the earth they must be carried out by human hands under earthly conditions. You must also know that these missions are often executed against the greatest difficulties, which must be conquered by spiritual power and devotion. It happened that this lama had partly fulfilled his mission when he became ill and lost consciousness; in this state he was unable to convey the entrusted mission to a fitting successor. The Great Mahatmas of the Himalayas knew of his difficulty. In order that the mission should under no circumstances be given up, one of the Mahatmas undertook at great speed the long journey from the Tibetan uplands to the Mongolian plains. So great was the haste that the Mahatma remained in the saddle for sixty hours and thus arrived on time.

He temporarily cured the lama, who was then able to entrust his mission fittingly.

You see thus how the Mahatmas help humanity, what self-sacrifice and earthly difficulties they assume to save the Great Coming Cause!

In this story of the hurried journey to Mongolia, of the sixty hours in the saddle, we recognized the same story, the beginning of which was related to us in India.

In Mongolia they called the Mahatmas the "Great Keepers" and they did not know which of the Mahatmas had undertaken this journey, but in India they could not tell us exactly with what purpose the journey had been undertaken.

Such are the ties of Asia. Who carries the news? By what secret passageways travel the unknown messengers? Amidst the ordinary routine of daily life in Asia, confronted with difficulties, crudeness and many trying cares, one may never be certain that, at the same moment, someone may not be knocking at your very door with most important news.

Two roads of life are evident in Asia, hence one should not be distressed by the visage of daily life. Easily one may be faced with the Great Truth, which will enfold you forever.

* * *

A long march on camels.

Through the air rings again the song of Shambhala. Here are stony mountain passes and frozen uplands, but never are you left without signs of Shambhala.

Our lamas bend over a stony slope. They are collecting pieces of white quartz on the neighboring rocks and now they are carefully designing something from these white stones.

What do these complicated designs mean? No, it is not a design—it is the monogram of Kalachakra. Henceforth from far off, this white inscription invoking the Great Teaching, will be visible to all travelers.

On the heights of Sharagol, near Ulan Daban, on the site where the Mahatma rested on his way to Mongolia, is being constructed a Suburgan of Shambhala. All our lamas and we ourselves carry stones and reenforce them with clay and grass. The top of the suburgan is made of wood, covered with tin from gasoline tins. My colors are used for decorating it. Lime for it is brought from the Humboldt mountains. The suburgan shines brightly in the purple of the desert. The buriat lama paints many images and ornamentations on it in red, yellow and green. Local Mongols bring their modest gifts "norbu rinpoche," turquoise, corals and beads, to lay inside the suburgan. The high priest of Tsaidam himself comes to consecrate the suburgan. The Mongols give their promise to guard this monument of Shambhala—if only the Chinese Dungans or passing camels will not destroy it! Behind the suburgan the American banner waves. . . .

* * *

A day of Shambhala. A festival. There are many Mongolian guests. In front of the tent of Shambhala the lamas pray for the Blessed Rigden Jyepo. Before the painted Image of the Ruler, a polished mirror is placed. From an ornamented vessel, they pour water on the surface of the mirror. The water flows over the surface of the mirror and covers it with strange designs. The surface moves, as if living. This is a symbol of the magic mirror, where the future is revealed and where revelations are inscribed.

A lama, the guide of the caravan, binds his mouth and nose with a scarf. One wonders why, as the day is not cold. He relates:

"Now precautions are needed. We are approaching the forbidden lands of Shambhala. We will soon encounter Sur—the poisonous gas, by which the frontier of Shambhala is guarded."

Our Tibetan, Konchok, comes riding up to us and says in a lowered voice:

"Not far from here, when the Dalai-Lama went from Tibet to Mongolia, all people and all animals of the caravan began to tremble. And the Dalai-Lama explained that they should not be afraid, because they had touched the forbidden zone of Shambhala and the aërial vibrations are unfamiliar to them."

From the Kumbum monastery, a high lama came to visit us, with his ornamented tent and colorful attendants. He gave us the sign of Shambhala and told us that some Chinese asked the Tashi-Lama recently to give them passports to Shambhala. Only the Tashi-Lama can do this. And just now the Tashi-Lama in China has published a new prayer, addressed to Shambhala. Now everything can be reached only through Shambhala.

Again barren rocks, the desert. . . .

We look at one another amazed, for we all sense simultaneously a strong perfume, as of the best incenses of India. From where does it come, for we are surrounded by barren rocks? the lama whispers:

"Do you feel the fragrance of Shambhala?"

A sunny, unclouded morning—the blue sky is brilliant. Over our camp flies a huge, dark vulture. Our Mongols and we watch it. Suddenly one of the Buriat lamas points into the blue sky:

"What is that? A white balloon? An aëroplane?"

We notice something shiny, flying very high, from the northeast to the south. We bring three powerful field glasses from the tents and watch the huge spheroid body shining against the sun, clearly visible against the blue sky and moving very fast. Afterwards we see that it sharply changes its direction from south to southwest and disappears behind the snow-peaked Humboldt chain. The whole camp follows the unusual apparition and the lamas whisper:

"The Sign of Shambhala!"

On the gray background of the hilly desert something white is shining. What can it be? Is it a huge tent? Is it snow? But there can be no snow now in the desert. Besides, this white spot is too big for a tent. And why is it so distinct from its surroundings? We approach. Coming nearer, it appears larger than we expected. It is a huge pyramid formed by the drippings of a large geyser of glauber salt—a real fortune for the druggist. An icy cold salt spring flows underneath this huge white mass. A lama whispers:

"This is the sign of the third frontier of Shambhala!"

Approaching to the Brahmaputra you can find more indications and legends about Shambhala. Another thing lends to these places a still more realistic impression.

In these regions in the direction of Mount Everest lived the seer—hermit Milaraspa.

Near Shigatse, on the picturesque banks of the Brahmaputra and further, in the direction of the sacred lake Manosaravar, even quite recently several ashrams of the Mahatmas of the Himalayas existed. When you know this, when you know the facts which surround these remarkable sites, you are filled with a special emotion. There are still living old people, who remember personal meetings with the Mahatmas. They call them Asaras and Khuthumpas. Some of the inhabitants remember that here was—as they call it—a religious school, founded by the Mahatmas of India. In this court-yard of the Gompa occurred the episode with the letter which was destroyed and miraculously restored by a Master. In these caves They stayed. They crossed these rivers. And in these jungles of Sikkim stood Their outwardly modest Ashram. To the outsiders, who have not been in these places personally, this question of the Mahatmas is not conceivable.

But traversing the Trans-Himalayas you discover that there is not one mountain range but a whole mountain country with a peculiarly complicated design of ranges, valleys and streams. At every step, you are convinced that the maps are only relatively correct. Because of their complexity these regions remain not fully explored. The hermit, hidden in a cave, the dweller in a remote valley, may rest undisturbed.

Having personally wandered through these labyrinths, you realize the hidden places, accessible only through some happy "chance."

Old volcanoes, geysers, hot springs and the presence of radio-activity, offer unsuspected happy discoveries. Often next to a glacier, you can see rich vegetation in a neighboring valley, apparently nourished by a hot spring. In the barren uplands of Dungbure we saw boiling springs and next to them magnificent vegetation. Strawberries, hyacinths and many other flowers were in bloom. There are several such valleys in the Trans-Himalayas.

During our camping in Nagchu, local people told us that to the North of the Dangra-Yumtso lake, among the open stony uplands, some sixteen thousand feet high, there is situated a fertile valley yielding regular crops. Near Lhasa, in some court-yards, hot springs may be found, which supply an entire household.

Having traveled through these unusual uplands of Tibet with their peculiar magnetic currents and electric phenomena, and having listened to witnesses and having also ourselves witnessed much, one feels one knows much about the Mahatmas.

I do not wish to persuade anybody of the existence of the Mahatmas. A great many people have seen Them, have talked to Them, have received letters and material objects from Them.

If someone asks in ignorance: "But, is it not a myth?" advise them to study the book of Prof. Zelinsky of the Warsaw University on "The Reality of the Origin of the Grecian Myths."

But after all, do not try to convince people. Real knowledge will only enter open doors. If prejudice exists, it must be outgrown through inner development.

For us it is important to prove, by the existing facts, over what immense distances one living consciousness exists, and how strongly this consciousness is open, ready for the future evolution.

In the entire East, the deep veneration for the Teacher has surrounded the Conception of the Guru with a sacred solicitude and impregnability. The conception of the Guru-Teacher is understood with similar veneration only in the East.

Let me remind you of the legend from "Agni-Yoga" about the small Hindu boy, who had found his Teacher:

"We asked him:

" 'Is it possible that the sun would darken for you, if you would see it without the Teacher?'

"The boy smiled: 'The Sun would remain the same, but in the presence of the Teacher, twelve suns would shine to me.'

"The sun of wisdom of India shall shine because upon the shores of a river there sits a boy who knows the Teacher."

"There are conductors of electricity, and also there are unifiers of knowledge. If a barbarian will make an attempt against the Teacher tell him how humanity named the destroyers of libraries."

The foundations of the East are fortified by the conception of the Guru. What wonderful words and dignified gestures can be found in India in regard to the Teacher!

Many Hindu, Chinese and Japanese scholars know many things about the Mahatmas. But the reverence before the Master, which is so characteristic of the East, prevents them from manifesting this knowledge to the uninitiate. The sacred meaning of the word Guru, the Teacher and Spiritual Guide, makes the subject of Mahatmas almost unapproachable throughout Asia. Thus, it is quite easy to understand why many who passed through Asia, have not met this question. Either ignorance of the languages, or diverse interests, or bad luck in not meeting the right people, prevented them from seeing the idea of the most precious. You know how very often we visit museums or temples, but without special permission, we cannot examine the sacristy and the hidden store rooms of museums, where perhaps the most precious things are preserved.

In the East, one finds many stories about people who disappeared; and some of these stories are connected with the conception of Shambhala. I could even tell you the name of a member of the geographical society, who visited India in the sixties of the last century. Then he came back and appeared again once at an official court reception and then returned to the East. Since then nothing was heard of him, but evidence was given to us of his existence under quite unusual conditions.

One can mention many people still living, who have personally met Mahatmas. Truly this has happened as often in India as in England, France, America and other countries.

When we followed the stream of the Brahmaputra, we remembered how a Tibetan representative in Urga advised us to visit an unusual hermit of untold age, who lived in a mountain retreat, as he called it, several days west of Lhasa. The Tibetan insisted that the hermit was most extraordinary, for he was not a Tibetan, but according to what he knew, a Westerner.

And we remembered again how a respected inhabitant of Sikkim told us of a strange hermit living North of Kinchenjunga.

* * *

The circle is nearing completion. Again, we are in Sikkim. Again, the splendor of the Himalayas is behind us, to the North.

All eyes are attracted to the majestic white summits rising above the clouds, as over a world below. From all sides, the best hopes are directed to the Himalayas.

Kang-chen-dzod-nga—Five Treasures of Great Snow. And why is this gorgeous mountain so called? Because it contains a store of the five most precious things in the world. What things are there—gold, diamonds and rubies? By no means. The old East values other treasures. It is said that there will come a time when famine will overcome the whole world. In that day a man will appear, who will unlock the giant gate of these vast treasuries and will nurture all mankind. Certainly you understand that this man will nourish humanity not physically but with spiritual food.

On ascending the Himalayas you are greeted by the name of Shambhala. In descending, the same great conception blesses you. Shambhala will nourish humanity with the spiritual food, attained by mastering the cosmic energies.

Good news awaits us in Sikkim:

During our absence, our friend, Rinpoche of Chumbi, has built two more monasteries and everywhere the images of Maitreya and Shambhala are in places of honor.

Our lama artist Lariva is still at Ghum and has painted a wall fresco, a mandala of Shambhala, in which, in a symbolic stylization, is shown the secret valley surrounded with snowy peaks. The Ruler, Rigden Jyepo, is the central figure.

During these years, Geshe Rinpoche has begun to speak more openly of Shambhala. In a symbolic form he tells of the power of the epoch of Shambhala.

Rinpoche presented to us a book published quite recently, dedicated to Shambhala. In this book are collected the prayers to Shambhala, given out by Panchen Rinpoche, the Tashi-Lama, during his last travels. From this collection you can see that the Spiritual Ruler in Tibet issued a special prayer to Shambhala in every place where he stopped on his journey. This is remarkable.

And then came a ring with the seal of Shambhala.

A gray, revered Gur from the Kulu Valley told us:

"In the Northern Land—in Utturkan—on the high uplands, there live the great Gurus. Ordinary people cannot reach this land. The Gurus Themselves do not leave the heights at present—They do not like the Kali Yuga. But in case of need They send Their pupils—Chelas—to warn the Rulers of nations." Thus in the ancient sites of Kulu the knowledge of the Mahatmas is crystallized.

Before me are six paintings representing Shambhala:

The most esoteric is Mandala of Shambhala, in which

one may recognize suggestions of reality. On top is the Yidam, as a sign of elemental force, and the Tashi-Lama who wrote the very secret book, "The Path to Shambhala." In the middle the snowy mountains form a circle. Three white borders can be distinguished. In the center is a seeming valley with many buildings. One can see two apparent clefts like the plans of towers. On the tower is He Himself, whose light glows in the predestined time. Below, a mighty army conducts a victorious battle and Rigden Jyepo Himself is Commander. It is the victory of the spirit on the great battlefield of life. This is a new representation of Geshe from Tashi-lhunpo.

On the lower part of another painting is also depicted a victorious battle. In the middle is Rigden Jyepo Himself giving commands. In front of the Ruler are all the lucky signs and treasures predestined to mankind. Behind the Ruler is a palace and on either side are his father and mother. And above is Buddha. This is a new representation from Sikkim.

The third painting does not show a battle—it is a triumphant one, with many golden ornamentations. In the center is a large figure: Rigden Jyepo giving His blessing. In front of him, in golden relief, shines the Akdorje, the crossed lightning. Below are the treasures. On top is the Lord Buddha, and to the right and left are two Tashi-Lamas: the third and the present. In this latter affirmation is expressed the thought of today. This is a representation from Ghum.

On the fourth painting, one sees many warriors on

horseback and afoot, commanders and advisers, gathered round Rigden Jyepo. The painting is from Nagchu.

The fifth painting from Tashi-lhunpo shows Rigden Jyepo teaching several Gurus the commandments of wisdom.

The sixth ancient painting, brought from Tashi-lhunpo by a lama-refugee, shows Rigden Jyepo in the center. The back of the Ruler's throne is in the form of blue wings surrounded by flowers. In his left hand he holds the wheel of law and the right calls on the earth as his witness. Below have gathered all nations of Asia. By their dress one can distinguish Hindus, Chinese, Moslems, Ladakis, Kalmucks, Mongols, Tibetans. Everyone carries his treasures: one has books, another arms, another flowers. In the middle is the great treasure. The battle is over. The nations have been called to prosperity.

* * *

Now let us summarize these scattered indications about Shambhala: The Teaching of Shambhala is a true Teaching of Life. As in Hindu Yogas, this Teaching indicates the use of the finest energies, which fill the macrocosm and which are as powerfully manifested in our microcosm.

Therefore, are the Asaras and Khuthumpas related to Shambhala? Yes.

And the Great Mahatmas and Rishis? Yes.

And the Warriors of Rigden Jyepo? Yes.

And the whole cycle of Gessar Khan? Yes.

And, of course, Kalachakra? Yes.

And Aryavarsha, from where the Kalki Avatar is expected? Yes.

And Agharti with its subterranean cities? Yes.

And Ming-ste? And the Great Yarkhas? And the Great Dwellers of Mongolia? And the dwellers of Kalapa? And the Belovodye of Altai? And the Grail—Lapis Exilis? And Chud, the subterranean? And the White Island? And the underground passages of Turfan? And the hidden cities of Cherchen? And the submerged Kitesh? And the Suburgan of Khotan? And the White Mountain? And the sacred valley of Buddha's Initiation? And Agni Yoga? And Dejung? And the book of Wu-tai-shan? And the Tashi-Lamas? And the Place of the "Three Secrets"? And the White Burkhan?

Yes! Yes! Yes! All these have assembled round the Great Name of Shambhala in the conception of many nations and many ages. There are also the whole mass of isolated facts and indications, deeply felt in spirit even if not completely outspoken.

Esoteric Buddhism penetrated into Tibet in the seventh century A.D., but esoteric Buddhists had their strongholds there already before our era, on the slopes of Kailas, and in Northern Punjab, possibly in the environs of Kulu. Although science regards Attisha as the propagator of this doctrine, the essential Teaching of Shambhala existed of course much earlier, the origin being hidden in the centuries.

Shambhala, or the White Island, is indicated to the West of Himavat. One must respect the caution with which the approximate locality of this remarkable sanctuary is divulged.

Bhante-Yul and Dejung are also synonyms for the White Island.

To the North of Kailas, towards Kun-Lun and Cherchen, was the so-called Aryavarsha, from where the Kalki Avatar is expected.

"The Place of the Three Secrets," "The Valley of the Initiation of Buddha"—these indications impel the consciousness of the people to the same direction, beyond the white ranges of the Himalayas.

Shambhala itself is the Holy Place, where the earthly world links with the highest states of consciousness. In the East they know that there exist two Shambhalas—an earthly and an invisible one. Many speculations have been made about the location of the earthly Shambhala. Certain indications put this place in the extreme North, explaining that the rays of Aurora Borealis are the rays of the invisible Shambhala. This attribution to the North is easily understood—the ancient name of Shambhala is Chang-Shambhala, and this means the Northern Shambhala. The origin of this name is explained as follows: The Teaching originally was manifested in India to which everything emanating from beyond the Himalayas, is naturally North. North of Benares is a village, Shambhala, connected with the legend of Maitreya. Hence it is apparent why the Trans-Himalayan Shambhala is called Northern Shambhala.

Several indications, blended in symbols, place Shambhala on the Pamir, in Turkestan or Central Gobi. Wessel in his "Jesuit Travelers in Central Asia" refers to the Jesuit, Casella, who died in 1650 in Shigatse. The proposal was made to Casella who enjoyed the most intimate relations with Tibetans, to visit the land of Shambhala.

The many misconceptions about the geographical location of Shambhala have natural reasons. In all books on Shambhala, as well as in all the narrated legends about it, its location is described in most symbolic language, almost undecipherable to the uninitiate.

For instance, take the translation by Prof. Grunwedel of "The Path to Shambhala," the famous book written by the Third Tashi-Lama. You are overwhelmed by the number of geographical indications, so blended and mixed, that only great knowledge of old Buddhist places and of local names, can assist you to disentangle its complicated web.

Quite easily, one may understand why such a veil was needed. One of the Mahatmas was asked, why They hide so carefully Their Ashrams. The Mahatmas answered:

"Otherwise an endless procession from West and East, North and South would overflow our remote places, where, uninvited, nobody may disturb our studies."

And it is really so. Here, in the turmoil of the city, it is hard to imagine, how many people are searching the Teaching of the Mahatmas.

A learned lama, whose name is known in the West, told us about the numberless inquiries and letters he was receiving from France, England, America, asking his advice on how to come into contact with Mahatmas, and how to receive Their Teaching. Thus, again, reality and the loftiest attainments come together.

Not a mere Messianic Creed but a New Era of mighty approaching energies and possibilities, is expressed in the term of Shambhala.

Now, when each day we are overwhelmed by the discoveries of physics, or the power of oxygen, by the reality of the Great Fire of Space, when from the summits there is proclaimed the teaching of Agni Yoga, then we can in full sincerity approach our friends in Asia in the Name of the coming Shambhala. And with a happy smile we can greet the Great Future of Mighty Energies! The last call of our evolution is the imperative call for creative action, for enlightened labor, for achievements here on earth, without delay.

Our friends, the Vedantists have pointed out that the epoch of Shambhala, unlike previous epochs, which have been characterized by evolution, will be attended by a great evolutionary momentum.

The Vedic traditions say that the time is near, when new energies, mostly Agni energies, energies of cosmic fire, will approach the earth and will create many new conditions of life. The date for these energies is calculated in the forties of our century. The Brahmacharyas of the Sri Ramakrishna and the Swami Vivekananda Ashrams, confirmed this date to us as well as the whole tradition.

The Teaching of Life by the Mahatmas of the Himalayas speaks definitely of it.

Agni Yoga, in full coordinance with the latest problems of science, points out its signs for research into nature's elements and the subtlest energies. That which but recently was commonly known as the teaching of will power and concentration, has now been evolved by Agni Yoga into a system of mastering the energies which surround us. Through an expansion of consciousness and a training of spirit and body, without isolating ourselves from the conditions of the present day, this synthetic Yoga builds a happy future for humanity.

Agni Yoga teaches: "Do not leave life, develop the faculties of your apparatus and understand the great meaning of the psychic energy—human thought and consciousness—as the greatest creative factors."

The Yoga teaches: "With self-responsibility and in conscious cooperation let us strive towards the predestined evolution. But for this we must first understand the joy of labor, of incessant courage and of responsibility, realizing all our possibilities."

Pointing out, in most practical formulae, all different sides of life, Agni Yoga reveals to us, how near are the elements, and the most all-penetrating of them—Fire.

Agni Yoga separates the reality from maya. Agni Yoga revolts against "wonders," bringing the phenomena or manifestations into the realm of positive knowledge.

"One must learn the organization of psychic energy," Agni Yoga affirms.

The Yoga affirms boldly: "Let us be sincere, and let us discard all prejudices and superstitions, which are not fitting to the conscious man, who wishes to investigate scientifically and to acquire knowledge."

Speaking of the approaching influence of cosmic energies, the Yoga warns of the peculiarities of the nearest future. The Yoga addresses physicians as follows:

"During the development of the centers, humanity will feel incomprehensible symptoms, which science, in ignorance, will attribute to the most unrelated ailments. Therefore the time has come to write the book of observations regarding the fires of life. I advise against delay because it is necessary to explain to the world the manifestations of the reality and unity of existence. Imperceptibly, into life enter new combinations of perception. These signs, visible to few, constitute the foundation of life, penetrating all its structures. Only the blind fail to perceive how life is filled with new conceptions. Therefore scientists should be called to cast light on the evidence. Physician, do not neglect!" . . .

"Our Teaching strives to the realization of the perfect manifestations of Nature, considering man as part of Nature." . . .

"Obviousness prevents us from seeing inner currents. Everyone can remember how he mixed up chance with the fundamentals, forming self-assumed conceptions. The same may be said of the element of fire. Someone thinks lightmindedly: 'Our grandfathers lived without knowledge of Fire and they peacefully passed into the grave. Why should I worry about the Fire?' . . .

"But the reflecting mind thinks, 'From where did all the unexplainable epidemics, which dry out the lungs, the throat and the heart, come? Above all reasons, unforeseen by the physicians, there must be some others. Not conditions of life, but something external mows down the people.' By this way of attentive observations, one may arrive at an unprejudiced conclusion."

Or Agni Yoga calls:

"Agni Yoga is coming in time. What else would tell that epidemics of influenza should be cured by psychic energy? Who else would draw attention to the new forms of psychic, brain and sleeping sickness? Not leprosy, not the old form of plague, not cholera, are terrible; against them there are preventive measures. But one should think about the new enemies, created by contemporary life. Old measures cannot be applied to them; but a new approach is built by the expansion of consciousness.

"One can see how during thousands of years the waves of sicknesses flowed. From these signs one can make a remarkable scale of human decline. Sicknesses naturally also show the negative side of our existence.

"Let us hope that the vital minds will think in time. It is too late to make a pump, when the house is already on fire."

Agni Yoga says of psychic energy: "People have absolutely forgotten how to understand and apply psychic energy. They have forgotten that any energy once set into motion creates a momentum. It is almost impossible to stop this momentum, therefore every manifestation of psychic energy continues its influence by momentum sometimes for a long time. One may already have changed his thought, but the effect of the previous transmission will nevertheless permeate space. In this lies the power of psychic energy as well as a quality deserving special care.

"Psychic energy can be dominated only by clear consciousness in order not to hamper one's way by previous sendings. Often a casual and sporadic thought stirs the surface of the ocean of achievement for a long time. A man may have already forgotten about his thought long ago, but it continues to fly before him, lighting or darkening his path.

"To the shining ray, small lights are attracted, enriching it. To filth, dark dusty particles adhere, hindering motion. When we say, 'Fly broadly,' we warn of an action. Everything said about psychic energy refers to action. Here nothing is abstract, because psychic energy is at the foundation of all nature and is expressed especially in man. Man may try to forget psychic energy, but the latter will always remind him of its presence. And it is the duty of education to teach mankind how to use the treasure. If the time has come to speak of the physical visible residues of psychic energy, then consequently, reality has become evident.

"This means that people must without delay strive to master the psychic energy.

"The Fire of Space and the psychic energy are close together and are the foundation of evolution."

As an example of the vital indications of Agni Yoga,

one can quote a passage about the sequence of nerve centers. It is indicated that Kundalini, as the center leading into samadhi, will in our further evolution yield its place to another center near the heart. This center, called the chalice, is the seat of the manas and the center of feeling-knowledge. With the expansion of consciousness, feeling-knowledge leads to action, which is the main distinction of future evolution. The center of the third eye acts in coördinance with the chalice and with kundalini. This triad characterizes in the best way the basis of activity of the approaching epoch. Not an ecstasy that carries one away, but an affirming and creative basis is predestined for the future achievement of mankind."

One can quote from "Agni Yoga" many indications of utmost importance, scattered all over the Teaching, as a precious mosaic:

"Have you learned to enjoy obstacles?"—what a powerful consciousness sounds through this vigilant call! . . .

"Yoga—as that supreme span with cosmic attainments—has existed through all ages. Each Teaching comprises its own Yoga, applicable to the grade of evolution. Nor do the Yogas contradict each other; they are as the branches of one tree which spread their shade and refresh the traveler exhausted from heat. His strength regained, the traveler continues on his way. He accepted naught which was not his; nor did he divert his striving. He embraced the manifested benevolence out of Space; he liberated the preordained forces. He mastered his single belonging.

"Do not reject the forces of Yoga, but as light let them search the twilight of Labor unrealized. For the future, we arise out of sleep. For the future, we renew our garments. For the future, we gather strength.

"We shall hear the trend of the element of Fire, but we shall already be prepared to master the undulations of the flame."

Thus the traveler of life is blessed by "Agni Yoga," which had been given "in the valley of the Brahmaputra, which takes its beginning from the lake of the Great Nagas, guarding the covenants of Rig-Vedas."

Too long have human beings remained at a low material level—they must hurry to acquire the brilliant possibilities long since predestined. One is amazed on remembering that Edison's phonograph in 1878 in the Academie Française, was denounced as a trick of a charlatan. We can still remember, how the first motor cars were proclaimed impractical; how electric light was considered dangerous for the vision, and telephones bad for the ear. With such reluctance, mankind gets accustomed to new conceptions. Prejudice permeates the foundation of society.

You may easily imagine the exalting sensation when, amid the white peaks of the Himalayas, you receive the mail from the States. Among much news of great importance, your friends also send you the newspaper accounts of the meeting of the American Association for the Advancement of Science, and in which many of the best American scientists take part. And you see how a whole line of sincere workers of science, from the point of view of practical study, arrive at the same conclusions, which are so imperatively affirmed by Agni Yoga. Armed with aged experience, Agni Yoga speaks on a wide scale of the spreading of true knowledge. Agni Yoga proclaims the scientific foundation of the principles of existence.

And where do we find a response to this Call? Far beyond the ocean, in America, the liberated minds of scientists, unbound by prejudice, turn to the same direction of reality. The summits of Asia and the heights of America clasp hands on the basis of true research and self-denying affirmation.

Millikan's Cosmic Ray, Einstein's Relativity, Theremin's Music from the Ether, are accepted by the East in a most positive way, because ancient Vedic and Buddhist traditions confirm them. Thus the East and West meet! Is it not beautiful, if we can greet the old conceptions of Asia from our modern scientific point of view? If Shambhala of Asia has already come, let us hope that our own Shambhala of enlightened discoveries is also near.

World Unity, mutual understanding—these conceptions had seemed like dreams of an impractical optimist. But now even the optimist should be practical and the conception of world unity from the note book of the philosopher must enter real life!

If I ask you: "Let us be united," you will ask in what way? You will agree with me: in the easiest way, to create a common and sincere language. Perhaps in Beauty and Knowledge.

In Asia if I speak in the name of Beauty and Knowledge, I will be asked: "What Beauty and what Knowledge?" But when I say: "In the Knowledge of Shambhala, in the splendor of Shambhala," then I will be hearkened to, with special attention.

From my previous words you may see that in Asia the essential Teaching of Shambhala is a very vital one. Not dreams, but most practical advice, is given in this Teaching from the Himalayas. The Agni Yoga and several other books, in which fragments of this Teaching of Life have been given, are very near to every strong and searching mind. Some time ago so much was said about East and West, North and South. These were the words of separation. Truly, where is the real frontier between East and West? Why is Algeria in the East, and Poland, West? And will not California be the Far East for China?

Agni Yoga says:

"Do not divide the world by North and South, nor West and East, but distinguish everywhere between an old world and a new world. The old and the new world differ in consciousness, but not in their outer appearance."

I noticed with great joy that in the meeting of the Asiatic Society of Bengal on February 5th, 1929, the President of the Society, Dr. Rai Upendranath Brahmacharya Bahadur, stated that "The theory that 'East is East and West is West, and never the twain shall meet' is to my mind a fossilized idea, not to be entertained."

So above all conventionalities, above all separation, are to be seen some sparks of peaceful world unity. In the name of this peace of the world, in the name of peace for all, in the name of the unity of understanding, it is a great joy to pronounce here the sacred word of Asia—Shambhala.

You have noted that the concept of Shambhala corresponds to the aspirations of our most serious Western scientific research. Shambhala does not invoke the darkness of prejudice and superstition, but this conception should be pronounced in the most positive laboratories of true scientists. In their striving the Eastern disciples of Shambhala and the best minds of the West, which do not fear to look beyond the outworn methods, are uniting.

How precious is it to ascertain that the East and West are united in the name of free knowledge.

I remember the words written by a Japanese into the album of a Western lady.

"We will remember you at sunrise; you remember us at sunset."

But now we can write into the album of our Eastern friends:

"In the name of beauty and of knowledge, the wall between the West and the East has vanished."

An inextinguishable Light is shining. From the depth of Asia is ringing the chord of the sacred call: "Kalagiya"—"Come to Shambhala!"